TIME TELLS

TIME TELLS
Vol. 1

Masha Tupitsyn

Afterword by Felix Bernstein

Hard Wait Press | New York City

TIME

ISBN: 979-8-9864463-1-8

Library of Congress Control Number: 2022940866

All screen images captured by Masha Tupitsyn
Photo images by Masha Tupitsyn
All other images provided by the author

© Masha Tupitsyn, 2023

1st edition of 1,000, 2023, Hard Wait Press

Printed in Italy at Faenza Printing

Book layout and design by Jim Colvill and Masha Tupitsyn
Cover design by Masha Tupitsyn

CONTENTS

1. Time Machine — 13
2. Reunion — 24
3. The Year of Magical Thinking — 28
4. Interlude — 38
5. Green Scene — 58
6. Summer 80 (After Marguerite Duras) — 75
7. Alternate Endings — 81
8. Time Tells — 95
9. Time Lag — 209
10. Future Perfect (Total Recall) — 212
11. Past Perfect (Future-Nostalgia) — 228
12. While We're Young — 231
13. 2014 (The Age of Style) — 241
14. Timepiece (The New Romantics) — 264

Afterword by Felix Bernstein — 285

Appendix — 290

"Does it change anything that Freud did not know about the computer?"
—Jacques Derrida, *Archive Fever: A Freudian Impression*

"There are many events in the womb of time which will be delivered."
—*Othello*

For Felix

TIME MACHINE

"Pretend it's 1995."
Isn't It Romantic, 2019

The people telling the truth are also the ones telling the jokes.

When I finally meet L—a gender studies scholar and online friend—in person at a noisy East Village bar in New York City in August 2018, we resume our ongoing conversation about streaming TV. The one we've been having via email and Twitter DM for over a year.
"What have you been watching the past few months?" L asks. "*Felicity*, the late nineties WB drama." I tell her. "And stand-up comedy." L laughs and nods her head. "That's perfect," she says. "Of course you are. Comedy has the answers." By answers, I think she means the future, which in this case, is the present. L tells me Lauren Berlant is now writing about comedy too. This is supposed to be a good sign, as though I'm onto something.
When I get home, I google "Berlant comedy" to see if I can find the essay. It comes up immediately and is called "Comedy Has Issues," a funny title. Personified, comedy is an analysand—a neurotic transgressor with problems of its own. Neurotics, Freud said, are the reason we know anything about the world. Comedians are too.
Before television went online, days of the week mattered. *Felicity* premiered on the WB channel on September 29, 1998, and ran for four

seasons. First on Tuesdays then on Sundays. The hour-long college drama spent two years in the twentieth century and two years in the twenty-first. The past and the future, marking an end and a beginning. Noel, a self-proclaimed "computer geek" and graphic designer, is the only character on the show who regularly uses the internet and has a personal website—www.noelcrane.com. In 1998, Noel is in the present, a present beholden to the imminent future, the one that will cancel the past: the new millennium. All the other characters in the series lag behind, forfeiting the digital. Without cell phones, or even landlines, they prefer to show up unannounced at one other's dimly-lit, analog houses. Noel talks about Apple computers as early as the first season. His love is expert. Everyone else on the show only uses their laptops as word processors to write term papers. By the fourth season, the characters begin to mention being "online," but only for academic research. At the end of the third season, during the last episode, post-graduate Noel announces to Felicity that "the internet is dead." He is devastated. Jobless, the dot-com industry has just crashed, and for a moment, the imminent future Noel represents collapses. "Though technically still in the twentieth century, the year 2000 was a good enough marker to stand for millennial transformation," writes Douglas Rushkoff in *Present Shock: When Everything Happens Now*. The future quickly becomes an anachronism that might not ever come to end the present.

 At the bar, L tells me that my now-deserted Tumblr has always had an "antique" quality. This is not the first time me or my romantic views have been called antique. I press her about what she means even though I have my suspicions. I know it has something to do with time. With being out of order, out of sync. With me rewatching *Felicity*—a twenty-year-old show that was cancelled sixteen years ago—on my computer every night. Ten months ago, in November 2017, I went off social media, leaving my five-year-old Tumblr, *Love Dog*, frozen in time. In 2018, *Felicity*, a deeply romantic nineties TV show, also looks and feels antique. I can see this now, in retrospect. But I also felt it in 1998, when the show aired every Sunday.

I'm talking about the year 2000.
The Millenium

Felicity makes us forget about the future, now and then. What it values is emotional. Stands still. The look on people's faces, the sound of people's voices. What it depicts takes time: the slowness of touch, the duration of pain, the long stretch of a look—"the time it takes to get someone else," as Jean-Luc Godard put it to Dick Cavett in 1980.[1] On *Felicity*, introspection is a way to understand something, not a way to forget—what Ben refers to as a "time machine" when he tries to think of a way to return to the time before he sabotaged his relationship with Felicity. "The one moment, the turning point, where I blew it." The time machine that Godard invents to get to someone else is a train. The time machine Ben invents is cinema, a film canister containing a reel of Charlie Chaplin's 1925 *The Gold Rush*, which he hands to Felicity months later. A material object but also a symbolic one. Ben has roamed the city all night and tracked down a print of the film he

1. *The Dick Cavett Show*, 1980. In the interview, Jean-Luc Godard discusses his 1980 film *Every Man for Himself* (also known as *Slow Motion* and *Sauve Qui Peut (la Vie)*) using the metaphor of the train and the train station in relation to cinema, waiting, and love. Godard: "I use an image to go from one station to another one. You need a train. I think movies are the train, not the station. I feel myself as being more of a train than a station, and that's an explanation for why I am less

and Felicity were meant to watch together the summer before at Bryant Park. They will go back in time, he tells her, by watching the movie they never got to watch. To have the love they never got to have. To feel things he had refused to feel. "That's the moment I'd take over, if I could," Ben says, creating an alternate reel. Through camera work and editing, *Felicity*, steeped in the metaphysics of time travel, continually reverses time; revisiting and recovering what has been lost. "At this point many turned back discouraged, whilst others went bravely on," *Gold Rush* tells us, charting an emotional journey that purports to be monetary—the search for gold. Throughout the series, Ben and Felicity take turns bending time in order to come back for one another, hovering in the analog nineties, in the teleportation of silent cinema, inside the ethics of slowness,[2] while time outside the time machine awaits the future.

In an interview, *Felicity* editor, Stan Salfas, discusses the series' focus on slowness:

> "[The scenes] play very long because our sense is that is how you connect with someone. And have a sense of a real and deeper layer of emotion."

Time is affective.

    L doesn't completely answer my question. I flashback to an email she wrote in 2018, in which she noted: "This kind of resonance is also what I meant when I said your Tumblr posts feel synchronous." I can barely hear what she is saying over the loud music at the bar. A votive candle

anguished. Because I'm not waiting for the train anymore. Space is the time you need to get to someone else." In his September 20, 2022 tribute, "Jean-Luc Godard as Airplane." Jonathan Rosenbaum recounts a conversation with Godard, in which he added an airplane to his train analogy: "I suspect that the wisest thing Godard ever said to me came in our first interview, in 1980. 'People like to think of themselves as stations or terminals not as trains or planes between airports. I like to think of myself as an airplane, not an airport."

2. In *Here is Where We Meet*, John Berger notes: "In speed there is a forgotten tenderness." In his April 28, 2022 blog post, "It's About Time," Edward Curtain calls for a return to slowness, when "people felt time in their hearts." In January 2022, film and television critic Matt Zoller Seitz tweeted that when

is glowing on our table. The young finance crowd that now occupies the East Village is celebrating for no reason, mid-week. It's only seven o'clock but people are acting as if it's midnight. Wednesday becomes Saturday. Everyone has a phone in their hand while they dance and talk. All the interesting and varied human gestures have been gentrified, reduced to one single affect: looking at a smartphone. L's words fuse with song lyrics. I move closer so I can hear her better. No place is meant for talking.

By "antique," L explains that she is referring to slowness and proximity. "Your writing voice on your blog always sounds like it's from another time. A voice that isn't here but somewhere else. And yet, it always feels close, present." I squirm, crack a joke. I don't know if she thinks this is a good thing. I will ask her later over text to double-check.

An antique is something old, out-of-date, from another time. But also: something that lasts, survives. One etymological derivative, "to see," is prophetic. A vantage point most don't have. I think of the scene in *Dead Poets Society* when Keating, a high school English teacher in 1959, asks his male students to take turns standing on his desk in order to see the world differently. I think of *Felicity*, my time-machine. Watching it then, watching it now. Up late summer nights in 2018 searching for random fragments of the series on YouTube. Not sleeping because the internet makes it impossible to know when to sleep and when to stop searching. Not sleeping because of the heat. Not sleeping because of the noise. Not sleeping because I can't let go of the past or because mourning the

he interviewed the late Peter Bogdanovich in 2003 about his work on *The Sopranos*—another late 90s TV series—Bogdanovich told Seitz that, as a filmmaker, what separated [*The Sopranos*] from almost every other show TV show was its "willingness to stay on a wide shot, to not cut, and to stay on people listening."

past is the only way I can face the future, which is always Now, and therefore never comes. August. Burning up in bed. The hum of the fan on top of the rattle of the AC. Grainy footage of ecru walls inside my laptop screen. Ben's dark apartment. Felicity's dark dorm room. The fake NYU campus is a California studio lot posing as New York. Stock footage of an exterior shot of Soho's iconic Dean & DeLuca (closed in 2019) is used over and over for four years. In the show, Ben and Felicity go back and forth to each other's apartments at all hours just to tell each other something. She is in fake Manhattan; he is somewhere in fake Brooklyn. Yet the fantasy sets make the enclosed intimacy between them more real.

On *Felicity*, distance is never an issue. Emotionally or physically. The city isn't true but the feelings are. The show understands that anything real must be done face-to-face. Which is time-consuming and risky. Ben and Felicity are the same color: two headlights signaling at one another—what Felicity refers to in one episode as "this force between us." Almost spiritual. Like the famous kissing scene in *Pretty in Pink* that the cinematographer Tak Fujimoto lit entirely with car headlights. Is this an accident, or what people look like when they are designed for each other? Lit for each other. I'm exhausted but want to take the time to look at these two faces again, so close together in these old, slow-motion scenes. The high-stake looks, the choked-up voices.[3] Words that take thought and labor. That take years.

3. Ben's voice has famously been mocked for being too quiet, to the point of inaudibility at times. In interviews, Scott Speedman, the actor who plays Ben, even jokes about his "mumbling" on the show. I would argue that Ben's tendency to whisper represents a tentativeness, vulnerability, and responsibility with words, which he takes very seriously, to the point of mistrust. He would rather say nothing than engage in small talk. In one Season 4 episode, Ben delivers a beautiful monologue to Felicity's mother in order to prove his worth as a romantic partner to her daughter. At the end of his speech, Ben tells her: "That's about as much I've ever said in one time in my entire life, so I'm just gonna stop," suggesting that though he has trouble expressing himself, he can force himself to speak when necessary.

When Ben and Felicity kiss, they always anchor each other's faces to make their kisses last longer. I remember the lore around the kiss in *Pretty in Pink* when I was a child. The teenagers I knew would talk about how "long" the kiss was—one minute, five minutes, "forever." You couldn't check on YouTube; you had to believe them. You had to wait and see it for yourself. This was before I ever saw the movie. This was before you could cheat time by living in advance.

YouTube uploads, bootleg copies, low resolution. Distorted, often inaudible sound. Headphones, no headphones. One day a clip is online, the next day it is taken down. Next clip. Autoplay. I reroute. Search again. Read the wildfire comments. On and on. I rephrase the search. Until, as if finally unraveling an anagram, I find what I am looking for—what I have suspected all along—by using the right combination of words. Mashups, fan videos, user comments—hate and love—mounting then halting at some point for no discernible reason. Why does it stop? Time stamps. Expirations. Dates on top of dates. The past coded, continuously uploaded into the constant-present. If this were weather, something we could feel outside, it would be a tempest. We would take cover. I click my way back. Now and then. Then and now. The past is an infomercial. Can we buy it back? The Google economy is the impossible rate at which we now breathe or can't breathe or have the breath choked out of us.[4] What are we still breathing for? Watching for?

4. Along with the groundwork laid by decades of financial absolutism, the COVID-regime has rewritten the core metaphysical coordinates of life. With the government and medical regulation of breath, we now have to ask ourselves: What are we *still* breathing for? And do we still have our sovereign breathing rights? In Franco Berardi's *Breathing*, he writes: "Our contemporary culture of breathlessness… physical and psychological breathlessness is everywhere." In her 2011 memoir, *I'm Over All That and Other Confessions*, Shirley MacLaine writes that she developed asthma "during the 'W' administration." MacLaine was so "frustrated with his idiocy and perpetration of harm that [she] literally couldn't breathe." She "felt the land of the free was becoming asphyxiated, too."

Do I have the language for this? Is there language for this? "I wish I had instead of words and their rhythms a cutting room, equipped with an Avid, a digital editing system on which I could touch a key and collapse the sequence of time, show you simultaneously all the frames of memory that come to me now, let you pick the takes," writes Joan Didion in *The Year of Magical Thinking*, yearning for the computer to delete the emotional hard drive of her grief.[5]

Everyone tells me that time doesn't change what the world is like—only everything else. To think so is nostalgic, inaccurate. So what is changing it? What has changed it? What changes the

5. In *The Work of Mourning*, Jacques Derrida recounts how his friend the philosopher Francois Lyotard introduced him to a word processor. Chris Marker's 1997 *Immemory*, his first CD-ROM project, seems important to mention alongside Derrida's *Archive Fever* and Lyotard's introduction to using word processors. Marker's later works explored the emotional and temporal effects of computers, multimedia, and non-linearity, moving between documentary and fiction. The analog photograph was once also a kind of hard drive of memory recall. In "The Article," Hervé Guibert writes: "I pick up a book of photographs and look at the pictures. It soothes me, as if I had suddenly and by magic entered a landscape, but without any of the inconveniences of a real landscape, without the bad weather or the insects, without the stress, without any change whatsoever. A total equilibrium that anesthetizes my nerves."

world? While visiting Lisbon on holiday in *Here Is Where We Meet*, John Berger realizes that the Portuguese *saudade* does not mean nostalgia but rather, "the feeling of fury at having to hear the words *too late* pronounced too calmly." It is anger at a too-casual dismissal of the past. Loss is not the same thing as change and change is not the same thing as progress. In *Present Shock*, Rushkoff notes that "change is changing, too." "No longer flowing top down, but in every direction," Mark McDonald of IT research and advisory company Gartner, explains. "Change will soon be continuous . . . happening all the time," states Dave Gray of the social media consultancy Dachis Group.[6] In the no-time and no-end of the computer, what does the saying, "timing is everything" mean? There is no longer a clock at the center of time. No time at the center of our lives.

"The point is that time is not neutral. Hours and minutes are not generic, but specific," Rushkoff writes.

I am not simply watching *Felicity* again, I am remembering time—a specific time—because it is over. The hours, days of the week, out of order. The Wednesday at the bar with L turned into a Saturday. Why does it matter? It matters. No more time. No more mystery. No more behind-the-scenes. No more that's fiction and this is real. No more that is in front of the camera and this is behind the camera. No more that was then this is now. No more hands on a clock. No more face-to-face. No more things you can't see but know are there. No more beginning, middle, and end. No more remembering. No more waiting. No more counting the days. The years. Time is no longer

6. Rushkoff cites both McDonald and Gray in his chapter "Digiphrenia." Also, it seems relevant to mention Simon Critchley's term, "counterfeit eternity," which he uses in his April 2020 article for the *New York Times* to describe the new Covidian order. However, I think "counterfeit present" might be a more correct phrase than "counterfeit eternity" when describing our current era of continuous media cycles. Or, as Mark Hurst put it on a 2021 episode of his weekly radio show, *Techtonic*, "the firehose of data." Hurst explains that "What these big-tech platforms and systems deliver to us is just *everything*. An overload of information and data and graphics and statistics for us to swim through… it barfs up *everything* at us and we understand fundamentally *nothing* about what's going on."

something you ever have to wait for or miss. Save. Get back. Show up and make a plea for. The way Ben shows up time and time again for Felicity. Time and time again for himself.

REUNION

Entertainment Tonight: How can we get you and Julia Louis-Dreyfus back together on-screen again?

Jerry Seinfeld: Time machine. Just get yourself a time machine. Or tune into a rerun.

—*Entertainment Tonight*, October 22, 2018

THE YEAR OF MAGICAL THINKING

In Season 2 of *Felicity*, creator J. J. Abrams filmed a standalone episode in tribute to *The Twilight Zone*. After *Felicity* ended, Abrams went on to explore the science fiction genre more explicitly in television shows like *Lost*, an extended permutation on time travel and fate, and serial blockbusters like *Star Wars*. The final season of *Felicity* was originally scheduled for seventeen episodes, ending with Felicity graduating from college. But when another WB show got canceled, *Felicity* was "gifted" a five-episode back order. Matt Reeves and Abrams, who was now working on *Alias*, decided to use the extra five hours to send Felicity back in time, giving her a do-over. The episodes "Time Will Tell," "The Power of The Ex," "Spin the Bottle," "Felicity Interrupted," and "Back to the Future" are all constructed around magic spells, time travel, and the alternate outcome of Felicity choosing Noel over Ben. "Love can be scary and can make you want to turn back the clock, no matter the timeline," writes Emma Fraser, "but Felicity always ends up with Ben—even when she picks Noel."[7]

From its inception, science fiction has been a genre of both magical thinking and failed

7. Emma Fraser, "When *Dawson's Creek* and *Felicity* Turned Genre," *SYFYWIRE*, May 16, 2018

mourning. Science fiction, like mourning, requires a lapse of time. The "future" is really a longed-for past. In melancholia, the ego is wounded. In science fiction, time is wounded. In his 1917 essay "Mourning and Melancholia," Freud writes that time plays a critical role in differentiating between the two states. In the memoir *The Year of Magical Thinking*, the momentum and force of Joan Didion's grief produces an alternate reality in which the impossible—time travel—becomes possible. Heartbreak turns into science fiction. Didion calls this magical thinking, which began when her husband John Gregory Dunne died suddenly from a cardiac arrest in their New York apartment. In the memoir, it is this longing—this searing wish—for the return of the beloved, a lost object, that turns time. That turns mourning into magic. Grief is a time machine that recovers the past in the form of the future.[8] In order to invent the future, we must return to the past.

As a genre of grief, science fiction revolves around the desired return of a lost object.[9] "Bringing [John] back had been through those months my hidden focus, a magic trick," writes Didion. In the documentary, *Joan Didion: The Center Will Not Hold*, Tony Dunne, John Dunne's nephew, recalls that when Didion told him she planned to keep Dunne's clothes, in case he came back from the dead, "it did not seem far-fetched. It seemed plausible."

Grief collapses time and space.

In 2005 Didion will write two memoirs about death. In them, she will turn back the clock in an effort to bring back the dead.[10] "In another

8. In *Gilles Deleuze's Time Machine*, David Rodowick writes that Chris Marker's *La Jetée* "depicts a not-so-distant future where a prisoner of war is subjected to a series of painful experiences that enable him to 'travel' in time. Whether this passage is actual and physical, or mental and spiritual, is ambiguous. Movement, drained from the image and divorced from the representation of action, has relinquished its role as the measure of time."

9. Some of the best examples of science fiction as mourning are: *Vertigo*, *La Jetée*, *Solaris*, *Starman*, *The Terminator*, Barbara Hammer's exquisite *Bent Time*, *Peggy Sue Got Married*, *Highlander*, *Flatliners*, *Until the End of the World*, *Waking the Dead*, *A.I. Artificial Intelligence*, *Donnie Darko*, *Minority Report*, *Eternal Sunshine of the Spotless Mind*, *2046*, *Inception*, *Moon*, *Looper*, *Before Midnight*,

world," writes Didion, "was the phrase that would not leave my mind . . . The way you got sideswiped was by going back." The way you go back is by getting sideswiped.

In *The Year of Magical Thinking*, Didion retroactively forms a link between her marriage to Dunne and the figments and trickeries in the lovesick plot of Hitchcock's *Vertigo*, a film that Chris Marker described as a work of time travel, and which he watched over and over again.[11] In her memoir, Didion recounts traversing time zones in 1968. She remembers flying with PSA—the Pacific Southwest intrastate commuter airline in operation between 1949 and 1988—which Dunne and Didion took frequently to see each other. In the future, when Dunne dies, Didion asks herself: "I was trying to work out what time it had been when he died and whether it was that time yet in Los Angeles. (Was there time to go back? Could we have made a different ending on Pacific time?)."

Is *Vertigo* an example of magical thinking?

In *The Year of Magical Thinking*, *Vertigo* doubles as Didion's lost marriage. Didion goes looking for Dunne in the past, which is *Vertigo*, a movie in which a female double—a time portal—opens up an alternate world for Scottie, a San Francisco detective. Some of the locations in *Vertigo* are places Didion frequented with Dunne when they were first married. When Dunne was still alive. The Mission San Juan Bautista, featured in *Vertigo*, is where Didion and Dunne got married. "We were married at San Juan Bautista. On a January afternoon where the blossoms were

which contains a speech about a time machine in the final scene, *Gravity*, and *Annihilation*. In an interview with *Film Comment* about her own sci-fi venture, *High Life* (2018), Claire Denis stated: "In space, time is so important." In a 2021 interview, Scottish musician, singer-songwriter, and producer Midge Ure stated that with the retro-futurist *Blade Runner* (1982) "you don't know whether its set in the future or the past."

10. *Vertigo* is based on Boileau-Narcejac's 1954 novel *D'entre les morts* (lit. "From Among the Dead").

11. In *Sans Soleil* (1983), Chris Marker refers to Hitchcock's *Vertigo* as the only film that "was capable of portraying impossible memory; insane memory. In the spiral of the titles, he saw time covering a field ever wider as it moved away ... this vertigo of space and reality

showing in the orchards off 101. When there were still orchards off 101." Ernie's, a restaurant that Didion notes no longer exists, is where "James Stewart first sees Kim Novak," who plays Madeleine and Judy. Ernie's is "our place," Judy tells Scottie. Ernie's is also Didion and Dunne's place.

In *The Year of Magical Thinking*, Dunne takes the "Midnight Flyer" from Los Angeles to San Francisco in 1968 to have dinner with Didion, who is working on assignment. Space and time collapse. The airplane is a time machine,[12] but so is *Vertigo*, which becomes a way for Didion to return to the early days of her present-day marriage before it was interrupted by death in the future. The film is a doorway to time. In *Difference and Repetition*, Gilles Deleuze writes that "A book of philosophy should be in part a very particular species of detective novel, in part a science fiction."

Vertigo and *Magical Thinking* are both.

But why does Didion lay her story (the story of her marriage to Dunne, a love story) beside the story of *Vertigo* (the story of death, madness, and grief)? Is it because death is a wormhole that splits the past in two? Science fiction, a form of magical thinking, permits us to travel to different time zones as though time itself were the lost object. Mourning, Freud writes, involves the long and painful work of withdrawal. "Its function is to detach the survivors' memories and hopes from the dead."

Science fiction shows us where we end up—where we *travel* to—when we can't let go. When

stands for the vertigo of time." In Kent Jones' documentary, *Hitchcock/Truffaut* (2015), Martin Scorsese echoes Marker's idea of *Vertigo* as "impossible" when he refers to the movie as a "lost film": "All the filmmakers in the seventies were trying to find copies of it ... So it became a picture we were *looking for*." The obsessive, cinephiliac search for *Vertigo* mirrors Scottie's obsessive search for Judy, an impossible figment of his imagination. In a 2011 European Graduate School lecture, Claire Denis, whose *Les Saladuds* (2013) is, I would argue, a reimagining of *Vertigo*, made this insightful point about Scottie's character: "Instead of leading the narrative, he is going to get lost in the narrative."

12. In his 1985 song "Manic Monday," Prince sings: "And if I had an airplane, I still couldn't make it on time."

31

everything (restaurants, airlines, movies, and orchards) is reduced to a memory of what no longer exists. We call this world of loss the future.

Both *Vertigo* and *Magical Thinking* involve time travel and grief. And while Didion doesn't note this, both narratives span a year.

From the Latin word *vertere*, vertigo means "to turn, bend."

But what is being turned? Time?

And what is turning it? Grief?

An anagram of *vertere* is *verrete*, the second-person plural of future tense of *venire*.

What "*you* make or cause to come."

You cause it to turn, to bend. *You* are being turned.

    Madeleine is the idealized past, Judy the melancholic future. By moving between the two, by doubling them, both Joan and Scottie get "sideswiped" into "another world." By searching for her marriage in the movie *Vertigo*, a detective story as well as a science fiction, Didion is telling us—perhaps unknowingly—something about its enduring mystery. About its unforeseeable future. About what time looks like when you reconstruct it through the lens of grief. Through a restaurant that no longer exists. Through a movie, which Hitchcock said "either contract[s] time or extend[s] it. Whatever you wish." The two deaths that come in 2003 and 2005 (her husband, then her daughter) will throw Didion into a parallel universe of grief, one in which it is possible for the dead to come back for their clothes.[13]

    In *Vertigo*, Scottie, real name John, is also obsessed with clothes. With dressing Judy as the dead Madeleine.

    "And then I'll buy you those clothes" Scottie tells Judy. He means the clothes that Madeleine wore.

"And then you started in on the clothes," Judy tells Scottie. She means the clothes that Madeleine wore.

Is *Vertigo* a story of failed mourning?

"It is clearly not sane to go on, beyond a certain point, testing the rules to see if they are made of anything (magic, consent, words, divinity)," writes Adam Phillips in *Going Sane*.[14] In *Vertigo*, Hitchcock recreates a living woman using the image of a dead woman. In *Magical Thinking*, Didion resuscitates her dead husband using the living image of everything that had once existed—both real and imagined—before his death.

In his 1917 essay, Freud initially gave us two years to "successfully" mourn. Movies gave us two hours. To do what? To go where? Science fiction allows us "to go on, beyond a certain point," while "sanity keeps us in the realm of the already known. Living within our means."

13. When asked about the death of her son, Slade Morrison, in 2010, Toni Morrison told *The Guardian*, "They say it's about the living, it's not, it's about the dead." In 2015, nearly five years after Slade's death, *The Sydney Morning Herald* reported that "Morrison and Slade collaborated on several children's books and were working together on a book of ghost stories at the time of his death from pancreatic cancer in 2010." Echoing Didion's wish for Dunne to come back from the dead for his clothes, the Netflix series, *The Haunting of Hill House* (2018), describes a ghost as a "wish." In her paper, "Melancholy Objects," Margaret Gibson writes: "There are dead objects and then there are objects of the dead—those spectral, melancholy objects mediating, and signifying, an absence. As part of mourning and memory, objects function as metaphorical and metonymic traces

of corporeal absence." For Scottie, the dead Madeleine is a dead object whereas the living Judy is an object of the dead arranged to take her place. Echoing Morrison about death, in "The Imagination of Disaster" (1965), Susan Sontag points out that "Science fiction films are not about science. They are about disaster, which is one of the oldest subjects of art," making science fiction more a genre of the past (antiquity; loss) than the future (imminence; becoming). Disaster is another word for ruin, which is another motif for loss—what Sontag calls "aesthetics of destruction." (Sontag: "What I am suggesting is that the imagery of disaster in science fiction is above all the emblem of an inadequate response."). Destruction is often more melancholic than mourning precisely because it is aestheticized and fetishized. Sontag describes this fantasy of destruction and depersonalization as "wishful thinking" that takes on a "technological view." Wishful thinking intersects with magical thinking as well as madness and trauma.

14. What Didion calls the "shallowness of sanity" in *The Year of Magical Thinking*. She writes: "On the most surface levels, I seemed rational."

May, 2015

INTERLUDE

For my final entry on Tumblr, dated November 13, 2017, I posted a screenshot of an all-green title card from Eric Rohmer's 1986 film *The Green Ray*. The post was a signage, a time stamp, a move offline.

Rohmer's green emblem contains a proverb by Rimbaud:

> *"Ah! Que le temps vienne*
> *Où les cœurs s'éprennent!"*

> *"Ah! Let the time come*
> *When hearts are enamored!"*

Delphine, *The Green Ray*'s heroine, is heartbroken after a breakup, but Rohmer's emotionally ambivalent cinema never offers any solace for romantics, not even ones trapped in a film about love. Either Rohmer knew the world is cynical or he was cynical like the world. Giving the world exactly what it is.

This is called realism.

In the 1990s, as in the 1970s, talking was the cure. The constant emotional self-analysis on screen was intended to be funny and eye opening. Looking back, it is neither.[15] Rohmer's late films, like Woody Allen's early ones, analyze relationships to death. There is endless talk but no change in heart.[16] Talking about the "problem" of love replaces the belief in love. In Arnaud Desplechin's three-hour *My Sex Life ... or How I Got into an Argument* (1996), a hopelessly neurotic academic French man in his late-twenties tells his habitually crying girlfriend, with whom he has been trying to break up with for a decade, "Love affairs are meant to end. They always end. I need to be able to imagine how it'll end." These kinds of "humorous" pronouncements continue to this day in the films of directors such as Noah Baumbach, who are touted for their honesty.[17] Movie relationships enter a diagnostic phase. They are debated and dissected until they lose their unspoken value and power. Anticipated breakups and endings are the new horizon of modern romance. It is easier to imagine and wish for their end.

This is called progress.

15. Tanya Gold expresses this same feeling in her article about revisiting all of Woody Allen's films in light of his 2020 memoir, *Apropos of Nothing*, and the 2021 HBO docuseries *Allen v. Farrow*: "In retrospect, and only in retrospect," she writes, "we see him, and it is no longer charming. It feels, rather, like another betrayal." By "see him," Gold means seeing Allen for what he really is.

16. In a 1979 dialogue, Jean-Luc Godard told Marguerite Duras that

What does it mean to talk too much? What do the words replace? What did they kill?

In the '90s, Quentin Tarantino did with violence what Rohmer did with talking. Catching viewers off guard, Tarantino distracted and amused audiences with friendly, manic banter that inevitably led to sudden, brutal attacks. The jump-cuts from violence to humor, humor to violence, established a cynical continuity and reciprocity between the two. Moving fluidly between affable chatter and deadly sadism, Tarantino made guns and witty parlance interchangeable. His characters, like Martin Scorsese's, were sociopaths not because they were cold-blooded murderers—we had seen those before—but because they were funny guys who liked to chitchat and share their feelings before, during, and after a kill. The type of guys who had a gift for doing both things at the same time, with no real preference for either.

Masterpieces are often unnecessarily depressing and overly articulate, two marks of alleged quality. To be a loquacious and confessional man is to be considered harmless and transparent, Woody Allen taught us. Did Tarantino, famously versed in film history (another form of excess), learn this from the melancholic Rohmer, who repeatedly delivered his lengthy colloquial blows by steamrolling viewers with a numbing surplus of aimless speech?

When I emailed my mother the opening scene of the 1990 movie *Pretty Woman* in summer 2020, she replied:

> "Even stupid films used to be magic."

cinema "talks too much. But more than anything, that it repeats its statement, that it repeats something written." Anthony Mann, the great American director of Westerns and noirs, echoed this sentiment when he stated that "a film has to stay visual. Too much dialogue kills it."

17. In 2018, A. O. Scott wrote the following reassessment in "My Woody Allen Problem": "The Woody Allen figure in a Woody Allen movie is almost always in transit from one woman to another, impelled by a dialectic of enchantment, disappointment and reawakened desire. The rejected women appear shrewish, needy, shallow or boring. Their replacements, at least temporarily, are earnest, sensuous, generous and, more often than not, younger and less worldly than their predecessors. For a very long time, this was taken not as a self-serving fantasy but as a token of

In retrospect, *Pretty Woman*'s commercial popularity and lack of artistic merit offer something more insightful than Tarantino or even the great Rohmer. When I played the opening credits of *Pretty Woman* on YouTube in August 2020, I realized how beautiful the luminous white titles are—crisp window blinds snapping open onto the Hollywood sign. Yet, the predictable façade, a line of demarcation, appears like the crystal ball of Cinema. Then the credits, the destiny of names: his name (Richard Gere), her name (Julia Roberts), the name of the movie (*Pretty Woman*). The future of this movie's success—the future of any late-twentieth century American blockbuster—will come to rest (roost?) on these names.

My mother and I saw *Pretty Woman* together in the theater when it came out. We were on spring vacation in Maryland, on a friend's 1000-acre conservation farm located on the West Bank of the Patuxent River, where we stayed every Easter. We had to drive an hour to the theater. My mother would take me because movies were always important to me. I remember the fullness of the darkness around the car on the way back, what Iago calls the "womb of time" in *Othello*.[18]

When I remind my mother of these Maryland screenings over text thirty years later, when all the movie theaters have closed and may never again reopen;[19] when the only place left to see anything or say anything or live one's life is on the computer, on which I watch parts of *Pretty Woman* at random times, in the form of YouTube clips, she replies: "And you even remember where you saw each film." A week prior, a writer-astrologer friend had reminded me of the musical track that introduces *Pretty*

honesty, or freedom from sentimental conceptions of domestic love . . . A sensibility that seemed sweet, skeptical and self-scrutinizing may have been cruel, cynical and self-justifying all along."

18. In an interview with *Off Camera*, the actor Chris Messina also remembers going to the movies as a kid and driving home afterwards with his parents: "I remember leaving the movie theater, my parents driving, and being in the seat, and looking out the window, and feeling like the movie was still happening in me. Like there was a camera and I was still in that movie. I was still in that experience." In Tsai Ming-liang's *Rebels of the Neon God* (1992), a cab driver father invites his college-student son to the movies: "I haven't watched a movie for years. Your mom and I took you to the movies when you were little. Do you remember?" They never end up going.

Woman, "King of Wishful Thinking." The cheesy pop song, along with the band's name—Go West, a Brit Pop eighties duo—is an obvious homage to California, a place to vend your dreams. West is also the Future because the future always signifies the direction of destiny. "Technology belongs to the destiny of the West," writes David Farrell Krell in his introduction to Heidegger's "The Question Concerning Technology." Destiny, like technology, reveals the totality of beings.

My friend confessed that hearing the song again made her teary. Had she also cried the first time? I played the song on YouTube to see if it would make me cry. I wanted to know if crying over lost time, like crying over spilled milk, was the cure to the masked grief of the pandemic-present.

The crying scene in *Vive L'Amour* (1994) is seven minutes long. The crying scene in *Goodbye, Dragon Inn* (2003) is three minutes. The crying scene in *Call Me by Your Name* (2017) is four minutes. In *Broadcast News* (1987), Jane makes crying a daily ritual. Every day, before work, she sets aside some time to bawl her eyes out, which makes us laugh. In Mike Leigh's *Career Girls* (1997), the tender-hearted Annie cries about everything at the drop of a hat, like a baby. Tsai Ming-liang says that the crying face in his films is a revolt against "becoming a stone." Crying is a way for people to "rediscover their tenderness," making cinema—and the art of memory—a gift economy, or what Estelle Parsons refers to as a "gift factory" (as opposed to a dream factory). The movie viewer watches the crying face on-screen in order to remember *how* to cry. Viewer and cinema cry together, each crying over the other. These days, my tears simply appear on

About his own childhood, Tsai recalls: "I grew up in the '60s. Then, all people watched movies. It wasn't like now, where you have all sorts of entertainment. It was the golden age of cinema. I was born in a small town in Malaysia called Kuching, which had about a dozen theatres and I spent my childhood there, watching two films every night ... My grandparents took care of me. I would take turns going with one of them to watch movies. I watched old Cantonese films, those made by the Shaw brothers, American movies, Hollywood blockbusters, Malaysian films and Bollywood ones." In Toni Morrison's *The Bluest Eye* (1970), Polly Breedlove recounts her time at the movies: "The onliest time I be happy seem like was when I was in the picture show ... [The] screen would light up, and I'd move right on in them pictures. White men taking such good care of they women, and they all dressed up in big

my face. I begin to cry without even knowing I am going to cry. I cry without knowing what I am crying about. My tears know more than I do. "Those tears," writes Luis de Miranda, "give birth to our world." "If I want to cry," writes Lisa Robertson, "it's because I'm not a pessimist." "If I cry," Tina Turner told MTV in 1985, "it means that tears come with certain memories."

The next day, over email, my astrologer friend and I agreed that Richard Gere in *Pretty Woman* is Julian post-*American Gigolo*.

Julian the gigolo, Julia the prostitute.

One movie hustles another. One character leads to another. What if one film is a premonition of another?

Why have I come to prefer *Pretty Woman* over *The Green Ray*, the better film?

In my film classes, I tell my students to look past the movie they are watching in order to search for where the truth might be, regardless of the movie it is in. No movie or director has a claim on depth, I say. The good movie can lie, the bad movie can tell the truth. The good director, who once told the truth, can lose their way and start lying. A trashy movie can take things seriously,[20] a serious movie can ridicule and degrade. The viewer's job is to learn how to know the difference. To listen, to look. To look again. To look back. To sort through what is important every single time. The truth might only be one scene, one line, a character, a look, a sound. One movie out of an entire filmography. But it is enough if you know how to make it count.

clean houses with the bathtubs right in the same room with the toilet. Them pictures gave me a lot of pleasure, but it made coming home hard." Unable to cry over her son's death, Toni Morrison recalls what her long-time editor, Robert Gottlieb, told her about his own inability to cry over his mother's passing: "He didn't cry for two years after his mother died, then at some stupid movie he didn't even remember, he started weeping. He said it went on for two days, just sobbing." Australian director Peter Weir distinguishes movies from nostalgia, clarifying that films "remain outside of nostalgia . . . they're like little worlds that you lived in." In 2016, at age 69, Wim Wenders told filmmaker Michael Almereyda that his road movie *Kings of the Road* (1976) is specifically about mourning the decline of movie theater culture.

Despite their divinatory pull, the fateful time the lyrics were summoning back by divining forward, I couldn't bring myself to cry over "King of Wishful Thinking." My mother's magic words about magic had activated something. But what? Thirty years later, I googled the song lyrics to see if I was hearing them correctly. Why these words at the start of the movie? Am I searching for my own tears and the answers they might give me? I sheepishly emailed the lyrics to my astrologer friend as though they were some hidden clue only I was privy to finding on the internet.

> *I'll get over you I know I will*
> *I'll pretend my ship's not sinking*
> *And I'll tell myself I'm over you*
> *'Cause I'm the king of wishful thinking.*

My friend was walking on the beach watching the sun go down when I sent her the lyrics from my phone. I was standing in front of the Hudson River in Manhattan when I received her reply. Two minutes later she sent me a picture of the Jersey Shore. We swapped our nature shots, the facsimilies overlapping. The sunset. The sunset. The photos. The lyrics. The sea. The river. The beach. Everything all at once. It was August. All the grief felt electronic, robotic. Our smartphones make real life impossible. The reason for our survival (computers) is the story of our highspeed decline.

Is time just a feeling you can never get back? Was time the feeling that made us want to live?

When I hear the lyrics to "King of Wishful

19. For the 2020 COVID-19 virtual screening of the new restoration of Tsai Ming-liang's 2003 *Goodbye, Dragon Inn*, Metrograph's press release informs: "By the time the possibility arises that the [Fun-Ho] Grand Theater is haunted, we've already identified it as a space outside of time—indeed, two stars of Hu's original opus, Miao Tien and Shih Chun, watch their younger selves with tears in their eyes, past and present commingling harmoniously and poignantly." In light of Tsai's pre-video-on-demand masterpiece, the derelict Fun-Ho theater of *Goodbye, Dragon Inn* is a retrospective harbinger of streaming culture where the moviegoers in the film itself do everything *but* watch the film.

20. In 1978, Mel Brooks told the BBC: "All my movies are serious." And in 2016, when asked what kind of TV he watches before bed, Woody Allen told *The Guardian*: "Never a comedy."

Thinking" in 2020, they no longer conjure a romantic breakup. Instead, I can't help but think of a different kind of loss, more imminent and total: the end of the world. *I'll get over you, I know I will.* "The lyrics are an omen," I tell my astrologer friend. "Time itself is the loss we would all end up experiencing and reminiscing about on the internet. Everything from the past will remind us of it." I say this with the benefit of time and in light of the present. Now when I watch the opening scene of *Pretty Woman* alone on YouTube instead of in a theater with other people, or with my mother, this is what I see and hear. Is this the magical—prophetic?—quality the film has now taken on? Is this what makes my astrologer friend cry? Is this why I wince and turn away in pain? My search wounds me but also offers invaluable insight. Time has not made *Pretty Woman* a good movie, but time has proven that it is no longer simply a bad one. Thirty years later the film has an unintended effect: it reveals what we are missing. It chronicles the losses (as do all twentieth-century films now) no one was watching for.

Over Skype, I tell a friend who is quarantined in Europe: "No one on YouTube is reacting personally to old movies anymore. Now because of the COVID-lockdown, it's all about the music of everyone's past. They are enduring 2020 by remembering who and where they were when they first listened to that music, in that other world. Even the people who weren't originally there, who were too young, or who hadn't been born yet, claim to miss it."

We both agree that while music continues to "inspire," its future—like The Future—is over. It now lacks what Byung-Chul Han in *Good Entertainment* calls "a sweet being here." Music has lost its youth, its "health." The past is a panacea.

A young Nietzsche referred to modern music as the "poetry of the future."

Time is a sound much bigger than image. Like that line in Derek Jarman's *Blue*, "Pray to be released from image." Or the way Wim Wenders always films music.

I say, "I don't know how to write about any of this."

After my Skype call, I wonder if all the talk about music and old time on YouTube has to do with the brevity of a song; a deceptively negligible increment that conceals a length of time that is vast, lasting, and intense. Music is where we live in 2020 after the COVID-economy forces us into a temporal lockdown. Is the pandemic just a pretense for the habituation of loss?

On YouTube, someone leaves a comment about Depeche Mode's dystopic '80s anthem, "Stripped," a song I have recently been listening to again: "I switched to music," they say. Switched from what, I want to ask. Cinema? Life?

Listening to songs like "Stripped" is not enough anymore. I need to read everyone's personal memories of it too. The further down the comments thread I go, the further back in time I travel.

Is time the feeling you get when you listen to music? Is music the feeling you get when you listen to time?

Douglas Rushkoff writes that predigital music was how our bodies got coherence. I think of the congregative euphoria of stadium concerts, before cell phones. The ones all over YouTube, recorded and uploaded for posterity. The ones everyone, including me, is watching these days. This is what makes me cry now more than any movie—the way we used to live in our bodies.

Music is a memory machine, but cinema is an oracle. So is YouTube, a preordained analytic that has replaced destiny. Cause and effect. The so-called search engine gives us just enough agency and causality to think of the network of the algorithm and what we toss into it as some sort of alchemy in need of our input and direction; our frenzy of hack questions,[21] like a roll of the

21. *WIRED*'s autocomplete interviews on YouTube, where a pair of co-starring actors take turns "answering the Web's Most Searched Questions" about them, comes to mind here.

dice, or a shuffle of the Tarot deck, or wishing upon a penny. There may not be a future, or anything left to know about it, but there is always the divination of the corporate algorithm, which generates an answer independent of time—or in spite of it. A technocratic will-to-power.

Go West's upbeat song is *Pretty Woman*'s psychic *I Ching*. It forecasts the diegetic future as well as the virtual existence of audiences to come. Go West begins with a wish ("*I'll get over you*"), a promise of a change in fortune. Destiny. Edward is clumsily driving to his future—a woman he will purchase on the side of the road—in a sports car he does not know how to steer. Does it matter whether the movie is good or bad? Whether the song is good or bad? Whether Edward is good or bad? Can these true things still be true in a time when nothing is true? Can love still be gleaned? Can you feel the magic of time?

The conceit of *Pretty Woman* is business, not art. The movie believes in what it sells, not the other way around.[22] Both business and art are cruel and always come at a price. It is only love that is against cruelty. Love that makes us good. *Pretty Woman* spends a lot of money telling us a hyped-up story we don't believe but want to see come true, even to this day,[23] and now only in the form of music. Others say the movie is just a lie. We cry, but not because we do not want this wish called cinema to end, or because we believe in this wish we called Cinema. We cry because we never really wanted our wishes to come true outside of cinema, and now hearing them many years later, we realize what we've lost when we listen to music, and all we can do now is cry about it for a few minutes at a time. YouTube is where we go to hear ourselves cry now. To remember when we felt things. To spend our time retroactively and remotely because it's better than nothing. Because anything is better than this. Because what is this? We watch the old concerts—the ones we attended and the ones we didn't. "The soundtrack of my life." The once-young bodies of our beloved singers dart back and forth energetically across enormous stages, in front of enormous crowds, hollering, sweating, reaching for us while we lost our minds in the happiness of an analog throng. Music is the great heartbreak economy. At these old concerts, we achieved something akin to total presence. Real eyes, live hearts, actual bodies, old selves, listening in real time without the fortress of smartphones making copies. We were just there and it was enough.

On YouTube, the 1980s are evoked as the last generation of memory.

22. Recalling an interview with the head of ABC in the 1970s, Jean-Luc Godard told Marguerite Duras what the executive told *Businessweek*: "People think we make programs and that's our principal concern, but in fact making programs is our secondary concern. The first is to make television viewers." In Hollywood, the same applies to movies.

23. In her 1979 dialogue with Jean-Luc Godard, Marguerite Duras equates much of cinematic speech, which follows the speech of propaganda and the political discourse of power, with a "speech that sells, that sells its merchandise."

Is time the love of my life?

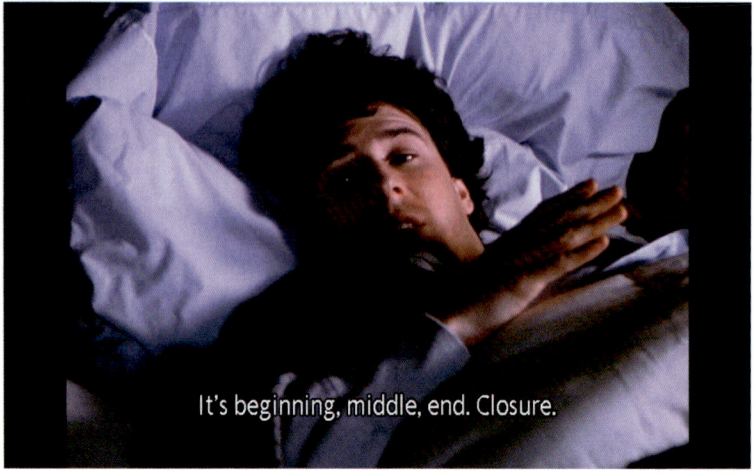

In 2020, people yearn to listen to what is gone even if they weren't there to experience what has disappeared, even if they weren't born yet, even if they come from the future. Music is the feeling of what we lost. But is YouTube a memory machine, an Orwellian memory hole, or a memory algorithm? The twentieth century's singer's voice prophesizes what we now know in reverse—what came true about us. To hear it is to know what was real. But is hearing it enough to change it? To want it back? The new world is an analytics of loss. To find it you must be willing to be its data. Its search engine. "It is 2020. Who is listening to this?"

I'll get over you I know I will
I'll pretend my ship's not sinking.

The thing you lost or never found is no longer simply a person or a movie but a time in which it was possible to entertain the premise that you could want to live your wish, the wish of life itself.²⁴ That you would be here to receive it.

Do these losses make every movie, even one as shady and predictable as *Pretty Woman*, magical now?²⁵ Is that what my mother means? Was it magic just to go and see a movie—any movie—with her, someone I loved? To spend those hours driving together to and from the theater every night. To feel so much time all around me, not just behind me. To remember it always.

On YouTube, Pretty Woman is more soundtrack than movie. Almost all the recent YouTube comments about the first scene are about Go West's song, not the film itself. Remembered time and imagined time interface, each intimately and indivisibly encoded into the other. Absence is ciphered as the memory of presence. Time is technological, but technology is personal. A place in the absence of a place. An algorithm in the absence of lived experience and firsthand memory. Is this a glitch, or does the Promethean gift of technology anticipate this glitch ahead of time, factoring in our searches—our futuristic memories and tears—for an embodied memoria? It is impossible to separate the two. Everyone is an intimate stranger. Everyone is lost in time. The more comments I read, the more the longing for time grows infectious. A bottomless Atlantis of old songs. Where were you then? Where are you now? Were you also there? Users recall dates under each video, more data. Absence adds up. "It is 2020. Who is listening to this?" "It is 2020. I miss this."

24. In "The Garden," Hilton Als writes this about wishes: "…are wishes even part of what's possible?" *The Paris Review*, February 16, 2021

25. In the behind-the-scenes extras of *Trading Places* (1983), director John Landis admits that his one criticism of the screenplay—a leftover, he says, from the cinema of the 1930s—is "the character of Ophelia, which is a complete fantasy. You know, this hooker with a heart of gold, who looks like Jamie Lee Curtis, and takes you in. This is men writing a script." *Pretty Woman* continues this male fantasy of the heart of gold prostitute as well as the tradition of men writing scripts about fantasy women. *Trading Places*' screenwriter, Herschel Weingrod, however, has a different interpretation of *Trading Places*' Ophelia, which could also apply to Vivian Ward's *Pretty Woman*: "Since it was the '80s, and

In his film cycle of Comedies and Proverbs, Rohmer sets Delphine's despairing wish for "the time of love" in 1986, four years before *Pretty Woman*. In Rimbaud's nineteenth-century poem, "the time of love" is cast into the future, where both love and the future will conjoin to become cinema. For a while, cinema is the king of wishful thinking.

There is no time of love without time. No beloved. No memory. No reunion. No cinema. No wishful premise. No world. When I greedily consume a year's worth of time by streaming an entire season of TV in one weekend—instead of by appointment or over the course of a year—gorging without pausing to take anything in; without pacing myself, without rationing or waiting, without leaving any time in between, I can hardly remember anything afterwards. The memories do not last. I feel ashamed. I realize I have wasted time. E. M. Forster: "Three years are not lived in a day." [26] [27]

In *Man in a Room* (filmed in 2018 and released in 2020), Paul Schrader states that any movie seen in a theater in the post-internet age takes on an aspect of slow or spiritual cinema because it requires a commitment to attention that home streaming does not. The same criteria may now apply to magic, which also requires a commitment to time. "It's like going to church," says Schrader. "You don't leave half-way through a service because you think it's boring." I think of the Picture-in-Picture feature—the latest screen-sharing and attention-splitting application that allows you to do "other things on-screen" (what "other things"?), while streaming a movie or TV show on demand.

it was that era of greed," Weingrod explains, "we wanted a hooker with the mind of a financial investor. We thought that would be a really interesting new way to try to deal with that." Similarly, high school dropout Vivian, it turns out, is also instrumental in Edward Lewis's (Richard Gere) corporate business plans in *Pretty Woman*.

26. "These texts could not have been written before they were," states the introduction to Derrida's "The Politics of Mourning." "For them to have been written, time was required . . . We will be asking about the force of time and the time of force . . . between time and the force of mourning."

27. In a 2020 Substack article on binge-watching *The Queen's Gambit*, angelicismo1 writes: "TV stands in a kind of direct and accelerating proportion to a certain *end of the world*."

In the 2002 premiere of the last season of *Felicity*, time starts to weigh heavily on her. Now a senior in college, Felicity still doesn't know what she wants to do with her life. She is afraid of the future. Her stride down a New York City street is played in slow motion, a leitmotif in the series. By stretching out the scene, by slowing down her walk, time—an academic deadline—is pushed back. The future in question—the one Felicity fears—is delayed and suspended.

In voiceover, she tells us:

> "It's hard to articulate this thing that I'm so afraid of—the future. I mean, why should we be so afraid of the future? It's just time. Isn't it?"

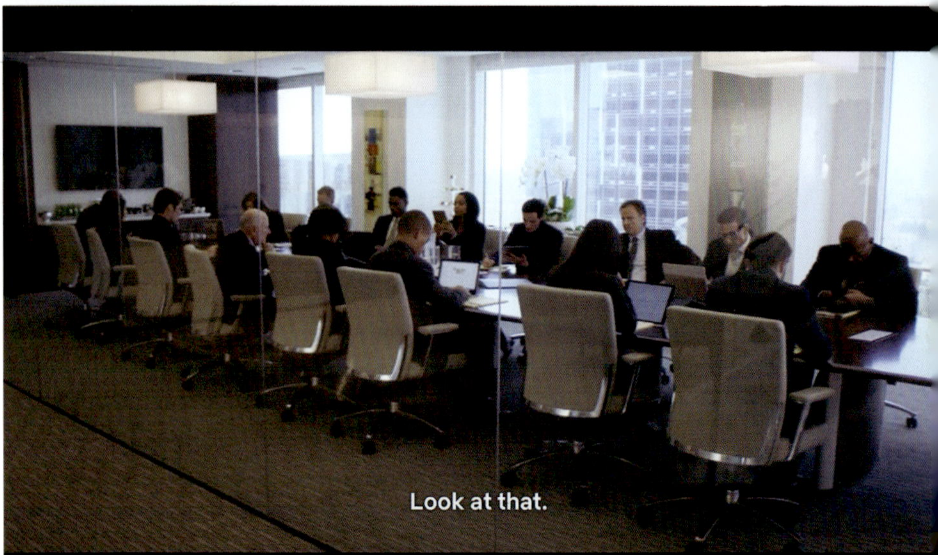
Look at that.

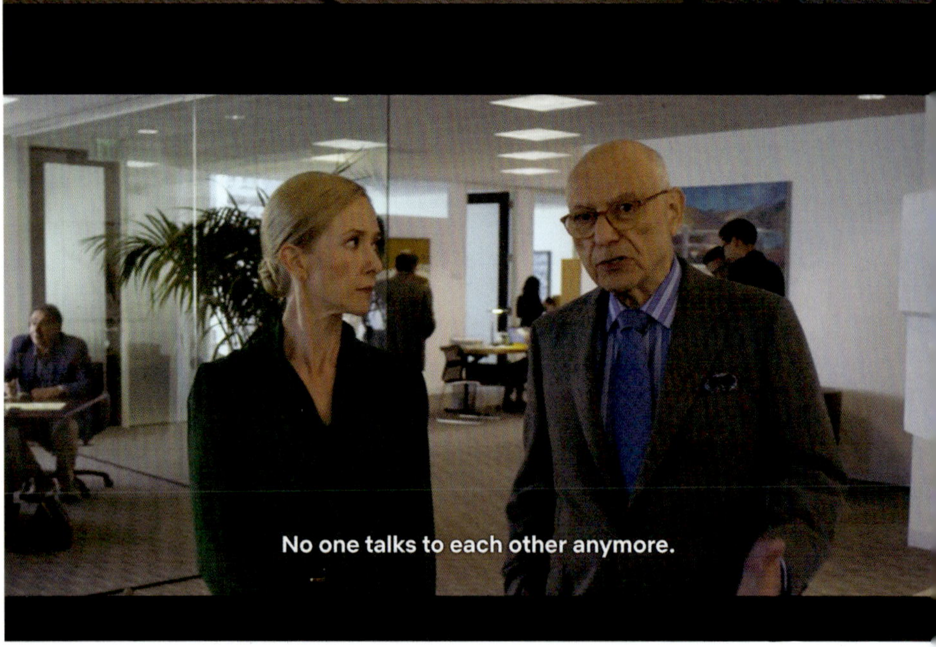
No one talks to each other anymore.

GREEN SCENE

- In Roland Barthes' *A Lover's Discourse* (1977), the word "futile" appears in a section called "Waiting." In it, he writes: "I am waiting for an arrival, a return, a promised sign. This can be futile, or immensely pathetic: in *Erwartung* (*Waiting*), a woman waits for her lover, at night, in the forest ...There is a scenography of waiting: I organize it, manipulate it, cut out a portion of time in which I shall mime the loss of the loved object and provoke all the effects of minor mourning. This is then acted out as a play."

- In *Call Me by Your Name* (2017), Luca Guadagnino also invokes the scenography of waiting. Waiting is a central motif in the film. In a pivotal scene, Elio waits for Oliver at the entrance to his house, where he can be seen waiting and where waiting can be enacted, made visible.

- In addition to time, one also needs a place to wait. "I was the first to spot him when he came into the garden from the beach or when the flimsy silhouette of his bicycle, blurred in the midafternoon mist, would appear out of the alley of pines leaning to our house. I always tried to keep him within my field of vision. I never let him drift away from me except when he wasn't with me." (André Aciman, *Call Me by Your Name*, 2007).

- In order to wait, one needs time.

- Seeing this scene, the viewer might think: This is what it looks like to wait. Timothée Chalamet's performance of Elio is moving because of its congruity: body congruent with time. Inner life congruent with body. Love congruent with waiting.

- Years ago a friend reminded me of the root of the word integrity, its fidelity to wholeness. The Latin word *integritas*, which entered the English language possibly through the French *intégrité*, is synonymous with Christian ethics: *innocentia, simplicatas*. Desire is made coherent by waiting. By waiting, by staying in one place, by not straying, Elio, a *virgin person*, approaches the full tethering of his desire for Oliver.

- "To be chaste is to know every possibility, without ever straying." (Godard, *Hail Mary*, 1985).

- The "play" of waiting that is acted out in Barthes' description in *A Lover's Discourse* is, in this case, film, which Guadagnino makes the viewer conscious of as material. Film is a space to perform—to act, to make visible, to see—waiting. Elio is absorbed, awash, chromatized in a sudden burst of green film that overtakes the waiting scene. As the green in green, waiting becomes the scene.

- "Suppose I were to begin by saying that I had fallen in love with a color," Maggie Nelson writes in *Bluets* (2009).

- It is 2018 and where has the waiting gone? Where are its scenes? What are its locations? What does it look like to love someone now—outside of cinema? What real hours do you put in?

- *Call Me by Your Name* is, in part, a recommitment to time. Audiences are moved by Elio's intense longing for Oliver, yet they do not necessarily understand why. They do not put how to put their own longing into a coherent form. What makes the waiting scene so affecting isn't simply the depth or focus of Elio's desire. It is the way the absence of the smartphone creates a time and space for waiting, which creates a space for presence and attention.

- Barthes: "'Am I in love?—Yes, since I'm waiting.'"

- The green scene is also the materiality of celluloid, of different exposures, the sprocket holes of a film strip disintegrating—what Guadagnino says was a "fuck up by the film lab, but also the miracle of cinema: 24 frames per second." In "Notes on Photography & Accident," Moyra Davey writes on Barthes' *punctum*:[27] "For Barthes, accident is the detail that wounds." Both Davey and Barthes pick up where Benjamin's "The Work of Art in the Age of Mechanical Reproduction" left off. The botched *Call Me by Your Name* footage is the accidental detail it hurts to see. The waiting scene wasn't supposed to be green, Guadagnino says, but the added element of aleatory woundedness; the double wounding in the form of a mechanical glitch—an accidental green—makes the scene the film's *punctum*. While he waits outside for Oliver to come home, Elio begins to recede into a giant pool of color. Elio's wounds of time sync with our wounds of time (in another time) which syncs with the disappearance of cinema. Guadagnino says the "fuck up"—his "favorite"—is about ephemerality. But I think it is about durability.

- "The ephemeral is not the opposite of the eternal. The opposite of the eternal is the forgotten." (John Berger, *From A to X*, 2008)

- And: "In the evening hour time stands still and eternity lingers." (Kierkegaard, *Either/Or*, 1843)

27. Orson Welles repeatedly stated that the greatest thing about cinema is its "divine accidents," or what John Huston called "fortunate accidents." John Ford, whom Welles admired greatly, also believed that the best things happen by accident. "Divine accidents," Welles noted, "are the only thing that keep films from being dead." "I would even say," he told Peter Bogdanovich years later, "a director is a man who presides over accidents." About Jean Cocteau's 1946 film, *Beauty and the Beast*, which was filled with numerous complications, accidents, and mistakes, Benjamin B. Dunlap simply concluded, "Some accidents were fruitful." (*Cinematic Eye*, 1979). On *Off Camera* with Sam Jones in 2016, Greta Gerwig talks about the rarity of "true mistakes" on film: "There is something very alive about them," Gerwig tells Jones.

- In 1983 Robert Bresson told French TV that he loved cinema because it is perishable.

- Is light also in waiting? In his 2012 eulogy for the war photographer James Nachtwey, Wim Wenders reminds us that "The heart is the real light-sensitive medium … not the film or the digital sensor."

- Hervé Guibert writes that photographs yellow and crack whenever they're exposed to light "too often. After a while, light always revenges itself for having been taken a prisoner—it gathers itself back." However bruised, accidental, and distorted the green footage might be in *Call Me by Your Name*; however much it hurts Elio to wait for Oliver like this, he endures. Stays put.

- Cinema of the 2000s inadvertently pierces us by showing us something and someone we rarely see in the digital Now: someone who cannot be distracted, dissuaded, defeated. Sped up. Someone who waits. Someone we can *see* waiting.[30]

- "… cameras, in short, were clocks for seeing." (Barthes, *Camera Lucida*, 1980)

28. In his 2020 HBO miniseries *We Are Who We Are*, Guadagnino embraces the digital: "I want to do something to be seen on the iPhone, iPad, computer and TV." Yet, according to the series' young female lead, Jordan Kristine Seamón, Guadagnino also issued the following warning about the iPhone to his young cast: "This little thing does not serve you. You serve it."

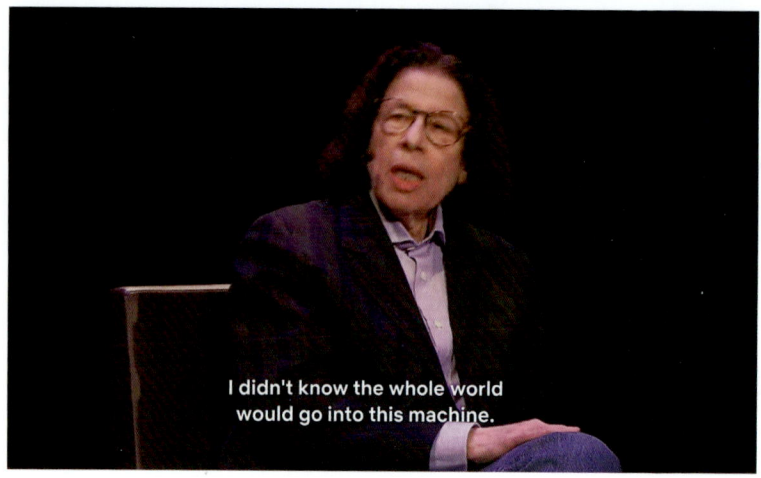

- In a poem, Fanny Howe, echoing Davey, writes: "While painting takes time and gives headaches/A digital camera doesn't blink and this produces a lack of analogies./It is not an open eye but an impure certainty./Empty frames stand waiting under the stairs." The green frames are analogies Guadagnino has decided to keep in his film.

- "I now know that there exists another *punctum* than the 'detail,'" Barthes submits. "This new *punctum*, which is no longer of form but of intensity, is Time, the lacerating emphasis of the *noeme* (*that-has-been*), its pure representation."

- On the digital Now, Douglas Rushkoff writes that the "possibilities of *kairos*" need to be defended. *Kairos*, he says, is an antidote to digital compulsions and nonstop choice-making. One might argue that Guadagnino's *Call Me by Your Name*, along with *I Am Love*, are defenses of the lost possibilities of *kairos* in the post-internet age. *Kronos* refers to the surface world, *kairos* the world of the senses. Like *eon*, *kairos* is the time of creation (Barthes goes further, calling the *punctum* the *kairos* of desire—the right moment to *want* and be *wanted*), the temporality of becoming. Guibert described the Polaroid as an "anguished race for immediacy," because it "[backs] away from time." At 85, the photographer Andre Kertész turned to Polaroids "because he arrived at an age when he can no longer wait for his film to be developed, out of fear that death might snatch the image away."

- When people go to the movies now, where are they hoping to go? What are they hoping to see? Without the movie theater, or movie-time, where is the place of cinema? Does it still exist?

- In an interview with Chalamet about *Call Me by Your Name*'s absence of smartphones, Frank Ocean observes: "And they had to wait to talk."

- "… and all we had was each other's faces." (Aciman)

- Waiting was once part of everything. We couldn't do anything without waiting first. We had to wait in order for something to happen. Davey argues that "the little screens that allow us to compose, rearrange, jettison," replaced the "phenomenon of latency" in photography. Is the previsualization of the digital work, *ahead* of time? Does this apply to people's inner lives as well?

- "We've learned to trust the photographic image. Can we trust the electronic image?," Wim Wenders asked in his 1989 documentary on Yohji Yamamoto, *Notebook on Cities and Clothes*. Wenders makes a distinction between his Eyemo camera and the video camera he uses in *Notebook*. He says he had to wind his "little old" Eyemo by hand, a 35 mm film camera known for its durability and built for twentieth-century wars. He calls his Eyemo a *She*. "*She* knows about waiting too." *She* had no stealth, *She* made noise. "The video camera impressed and disturbed no one. *She* was just there." *Notebook on Cities and Clothes* moves back and forth between celluloid and video, the photographic and the electronic, big screen and little screen, in the same way that Wenders says Yamamoto's clothes felt new and old at the same time. Wenders holds the miniature LED of the designer like a locket in the palm of his hand. In the future, a person is a monitor. A year later,

Wenders began making his five-hour global sci-fi, *Until the End of the World*, which he says would not have been possible had he not made *Notebook* first. All the little monitors everywhere in *Notebook* were the future, Wenders concluded in 2019. Yamamoto states that as a product of the electronic age, the contemporary designer, "can never stop" producing new clothes. "If he stops, he's finished." I consider the writer in the digital age. I consider myself. Did I "die" when I left social media in 2017? Am I "finished" as far as the digital world is concerned?

- In *Call Me by Your Name*'s waiting scene, the world turns green. Green is not a color you fall in love with, as Nelson tells us she falls for blue, the "color of poison," according to Caravaggio.

- Mark Zuckerberg, who is red-green color-blind, selected to make Facebook—a poison—blue. He told ABC News: "Blue is the richest color for me. I can see all of blue." He turned the color blue green by capitalizing on it, by turning it into money.

- Green is the color you become when in love. For love. It is "the color of my face," sings Sufjan Stevens in his track for *Call Me by Your Name*'s waiting scene.

- Writing about the Garden of Eden in *Chroma*, the filmmaker Derek Jarman asks if green is "the first color of perception?" The very first color Adam ever sees. First love, first sight, first color. What Howe means by "love is the green in green" is that love, which is green, turns everything green, even Guadagnino's footage.

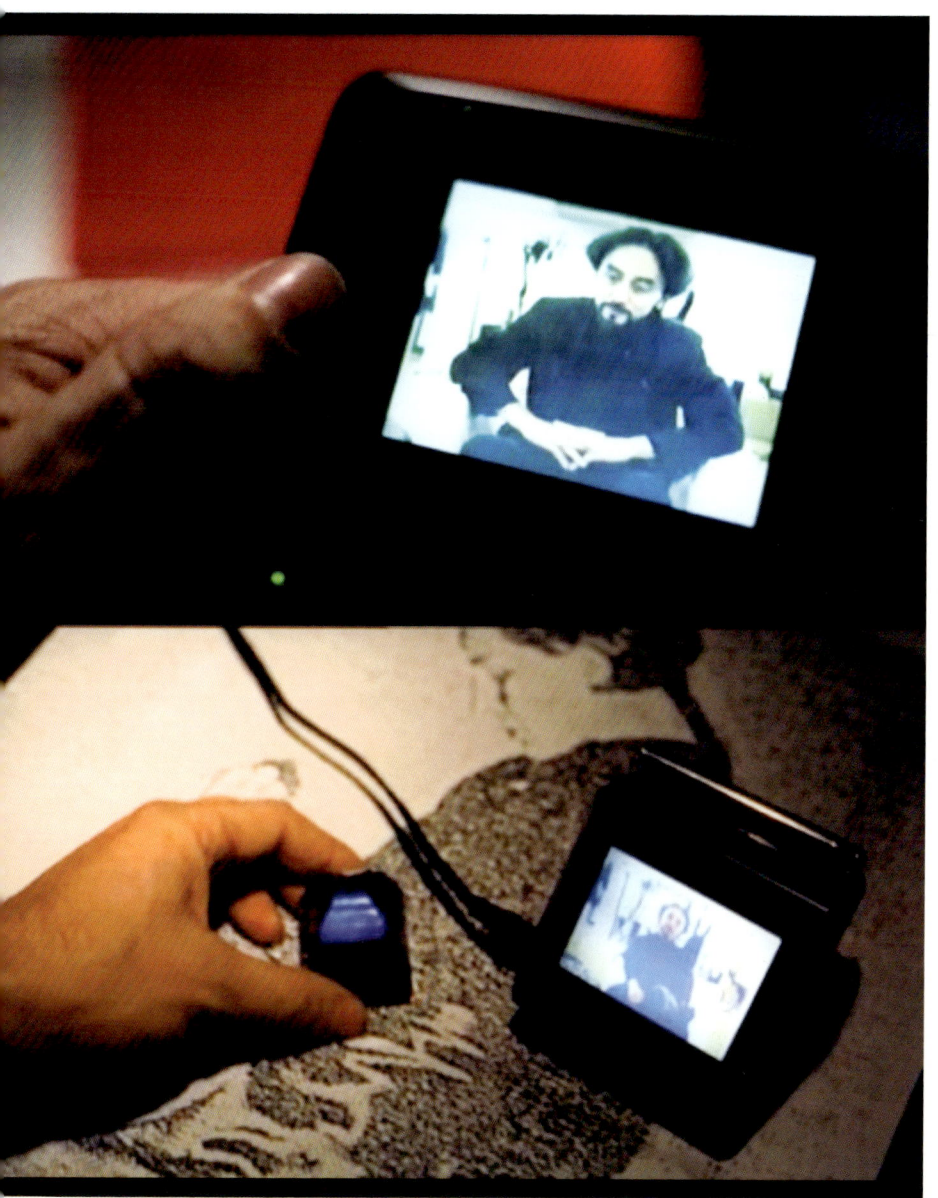

- "The Green Knight comes to King Arthur's court, his hair and complexion green, riding a green horse, and carrying an axe of green gold. He commands Gawain to meet him at the Green Chapel at the spring solstice." (Jarman)

- At the end of the film, Elio and Oliver go to Bergamo together for the weekend. After a close-up of the two sitting on a bus, the drive is filmed as an exterior shot of pure movement ("What's a bus doing in this story?" Guibert asks in "The Bus." "To me a bus is a big machine for taking pictures, a miraculous tripod … a moving and dynamic tripod . . . The window, which defines a succession of exteriors, is a readymade frame . . . The bus is a two-way picture-taking machine."). The summer green that is all around them becomes both interior (emotional) and exterior (*mise-en-scène*). The now-unseen vehicle takes off like a spaceship into a levitating forest. The emotion of the forest fills the frame. Elio and Oliver are flying through the green, as if they are themselves the green. "Love is the green in green."

- "Summer houses and temples to Venus are hidden in the green woods." (Jarman)

- If green is first, what is last? Blue? After the first love, does one ever wait like that again?

- Jarman: "Apropos of that green carnation, Havelock Ellis was certain that queers preferred green to any other color. Did they secretly drag up in all those emerald dresses that the girls had cast off? Hand a color swatch to a lad with cock on his mind and see what color he chooses."

- On my last night in the French countryside in 2013, my French lover's sister cooked us a homemade vegetable soup. The color of the soup was such a shocking deep-forest green that we both paused to look down at our bowls before eating. My lover, who was a lot like Oliver—shaky, weak, unpredictable, full of holes—took my hand under the table and squeezed it with uncommon strength. In my ear, he whispered: "Green is the color of hope."

- Barthes writes that "waiting is an enchantment: I have received *orders not to move* . . . I forbid myself to leave the room, to go to the toilet, even to telephone to keep the line from being busy . . . All these diversions which solicit me are so many wasted moments for waiting, so many impurities of anxiety. For the anxiety of waiting, in its pure state, requires that I be sitting in a chair within reach of the telephone, without doing anything."

- When Oliver finally returns, he is drunk and Elio, who has waited for him all night, is pretending to be asleep in the room they share. Oliver pretends that he is the kind of man who does not know or care that Elio has been waiting for him.

- What are we missing by waiting? What are we willing to miss by waiting?

- Rushkoff: "We must retrain ourselves to see the reward in the amount of time we get to spend in the reverie of solo contemplation or live engagement with another human being."

We chose not to cheat with the distance or the geography

- At the end of *Call Me by Your Name*, it is winter and Elio is the first to answer Oliver's telephone call. Four months have gone by but it is as though Elio has not moved all this time. He has been waiting. He only left his waiting post once, with tragic consequences. Trading the waiting scene (which he could no longer physically stand) for the straight scene: Elio had sex with Marzia, a childhood friend. Elio wastes Marzia's time in order to buy time for Oliver. Men kill time—*pass* the time—with women they do not love. It happens all the time.

- "... All I prayed for was for time to stop ... The agony wore me out in the end, and on scalding afternoons, I'd simply give out and fall asleep on the living room sofa and, though still dreaming, know exactly who was in the room, who had tiptoed in and out, who was standing there, who was looking at me and for how long, who was trying to pick out today's paper while making the least rustling sound ... By noon, the agony of waiting to hear him say anything to me was more than I could bear." (Aciman)

- "If you knew the number, you could arrange to be called in a telephone box. You didn't pay. You waited. (John Berger to Anne Michaels, *Railtracks*, 2011)

- "Telephone: His voice makes him visible." (Robert Bresson)

- "Wait here so I can say love." (Jackson MacLow)

- "One may now 'take the waiting out of wanting.'" (Zygmunt Bauman)

- "The movements of your phone are the movements of you as a person." (Edward Snowden, 2019)

- "He waited for the beloved to return. Inevitable that wait." (E. M. Forster, *Maurice*, 1971)

- "How long is your watch?" (*The Little Things*, 2021)

- What do you do when your heart is broken because the landscape is broken? No longer green, but something permanently—even post— blue. You watch movies to look for love.

SUMMER 80
(AFTER MARGUERITE DURAS)

"… and I shut you all in that bedroom lost above time."
—Marguerite Duras, "Summer 80"

At the end of *Call Me by Your Name* Elio receives a telephone call from Oliver at his summer home. Is this the first call since they said goodbye? I ask because of the magnitude of the blow. The crying credits. The hope that is crushed (am I more crushed than Elio?) after the long, protracted wait. The shock of hearing about Oliver's plans to marry a woman he has kept secret from Elio but also from us. The phone call casts doubt on everything we have seen, turning it into a lie.

Elio thought the phone call would bring a different kind of news. The news that Oliver could not go on without him. The news—after the time-jump from summer to winter—that the wait was finally over.

The news we all want to get.

During the end credits, Elio sits in front of his fireplace and begins to cry. His face suffers the cold blast of Oliver's words, which have come to nothing afer all this time. While he cries, a fly zigzags around his shoulder, jumping in and out of the frame. Death, decay. We were not expecting to see this anguish in one long take. To have this uncut rolling sorrow be the end. I think of E. M. Forster's piercing line in *Maurice*: "'What an ending,' he sobbed, 'what an ending.'"

We no longer expect cinema to counter our heartbreak, to amend a wrong, to turn back time. We are all Olivers using Elios half-heartedly—irresponsibly—for a summer.

We think: *it was good while it lasted*.

I didn't notice the fly when I first watched the end credits on YouTube, only on the big screen at a Multiplex a month later. I was alone in the huge ship-like theater in Battery Park where I watched movies every night using my MoviePass in 2018. Is the fly there by accident or on purpose, like the green scene before it? Is the fly a mistake, a *punctum* in this otherwise beautiful, unexpected image of grief?

There are insects in *I Am Love*, Guadagnino's earlier film. Insects while Emma and Antonio (much younger than Emma, the way Elio is much younger than Oliver) make love for the first time in the uncut grass at Antonio's Italian farm. In broad daylight, the insects traffic around the duo's naked bodies. Despite their age difference, Emma loves the way Antonio loves, so it is a match. The active buzzing is the score of sex. Emma and Antonio are in the open air, and insects belong to nature, and now nature belongs to them because love puts us somewhere *else*.

Somewhere outside.

Timothée Chalamet admitted to initially disliking Guadagnino's crying coda. "People are leaving the theater," he complained in one interview. "They don't know it's not over yet. Is it over yet?" Chalamet was referring to the movie audience but also to Elio, who doesn't know if it's over between him and Oliver. Chalamet's question echoes the signature Sufjan Stevens lyric that accompanies the end credits, "Is it a video? Is it a video?"

What ending is the movie audience walking out on? What ending are we?

We leave prematurely. We leave too soon. We leave when we shouldn't. We cut out.

In life, some people stay too long, some leave too soon.

Over dinner for a well-known writer at Café Loup (closed in 2020) in winter 2018, a male friend who reads my Tarot cards every year, told me that when it comes to romantic relationships, "One person is always an Elio and one person is always an Oliver." We had both just seen *Call Me by Your Name* and were discussing it. He was not reading the Tarot when he declared this. On my way to the restroom, I drunkenly mumbled, "If equal affections cannot be, let the more loving one be me," as a private retort. After dinner, while walking home, I also thought of E. M. Forster's *Maurice* again, his idea of sexual harmony: "Neither thought: 'Am I led; am I leading?'"

When my Tarot reader said love is never equal, I looked over at his boyfriend, who was deep in conversation with the famous older writer at our dinner table. I wondered if this was true about them? Over the years, on separate occasions, they had both casually accused the other of being an Oliver, insisting they were both Elios.

Until the winter phone call, Elio didn't realize he had been left, even though Oliver had made it clear he wasn't capable of staying.

Was it clear to us?

In the middle of the movie, Elio and Oliver visit Crema one afternoon. On this day they will kiss for the first time while lying in some grass. Earlier, at the Battle of Piave, a World War I memorial, Elio cryptically professed his feelings for Oliver. In response, Oliver gently orders Elio not to "go anywhere" as he runs across the street to see his translator. It is a test. Wait for me, he is saying. "You know I'm not going anywhere," mumbles Elio, who frequently talks to himself while taking a drag off his cigarette, hard-boiled. He is the much younger man but he is the older man. He is a weary character in a film noir, where the hardest, most reticent person is usually the softest and most vulnerable. The one whose armor always gets wrecked.

At the Battle of Piave, the sun is ultrabright, public domain. But Oliver's words have a Sphinxian chain of command. Oliver is a femme fatale: empty, staggering—built for no one. Elio is hooked from day one.

When Oliver first arrives for the summer to intern for Elio's father, Elio looks down at him from his second story bedroom window, a disgruntled princess in a fairytale rejecting the imposition of an unwanted suitor. He refers to Oliver as the "usurpateur." To Elio, Oliver has laid some kind of immediate claim on him. Uttering the word is intended to break Oliver's silent hold. *Usurpateur*, I discover, also means imposter, and *spoofer* (blague), which means joke, trick—prank in French. Calling Oliver a *usurpateur* makes sense given the way things will turn out.

During the movie's long waiting scene, Elio dozes in and out of sleep. He is sometimes startled awake by noises he mistakes for Oliver. He dreams of Oliver's return. But has this whole thing been a dream? Is Oliver a fantasy? A hoax? Did Elio imagine him?[29] Did we? Is this what men do, even to other men, when those men act too similar to women? My Tarot reader did not specify gender or sex or time. Simply: everyone is like this; nothing is ever really equal. He said this over dinner at Café Loup, and then again over text the next morning after we both had time to sleep on it. He didn't change his mind or explain what he meant.

Everyone is like what, I wonder—men?

The song that plays over *Call Me by Your Name*'s end credits expresses disbelief. The singer asks, "Is it a video? Is it a video?" Like Elio, he cannot understand what he is seeing even though he is seeing it; even though it happened. Because cinema would not gaslight us like this, but a video person in a video world would.

---

29. In Kierkegaard's *The Seducer's Diary*, the broken-hearted and dumbstruck Regine, a woman, is put into the same position as Elio. Kierkegaard writes: "And now, since the relationship had possessed actuality only figuratively, she had to battle continually the doubt whether the whole affair was not a fantasy. She could not confide in anyone, because she did not really have anything to confide."

The video exists but means nothing. The video proves everything but will never bind.

Write back, you fucking asshole.

I can't use a machine to write an old friend.

ALTERNATE ENDINGS

In February 2018, I DM L that I might be writing a new book. I am hesitant to tell her this, to tell anyone this, because writing is hard for me. I tell her it is the first time I have enjoyed writing in over two years. I say I have retired from writing "but it just came out." The statement, a proviso, protects me in case it is true. L DMs back, reminding me of a line I wrote on my Tumblr on October 28, 2017, two weeks before I wrote my final entry and deactivated my Twitter account. In the post, I wrote about the alternate ending that is included in the Criterion release of *Broadcast News*.

In the 1987 theatrical release of *Broadcast News*, Tom and Jane famously separate at the end of the movie. In the alternate ending, Tom gets in the cab with Jane in attempt to stay together.[30] The breach of journalistic ethics she has accused him of is not discussed, but the very act of him coming back to Jane, of not getting on the plane after her allegation, suggests an ethical address. In the theatrical ending, Tom waits for Jane to follow him. Jane waits for Tom to come back. Tom gets on a plane to the Bahamas without Jane. Jane leaves the airport in Washington, D.C., without Tom. The film ends with Jane crying in the back

30. I have recorded a video excerpt of the alternate ending of *Broadcast News*, 1987: https://rumble.com/vtfkqm-alternate-ending-broadcast-news.html

of a taxi. Jane crying is a leitmotif in the film. Tom and Jane go their separate ways. A seven-year time-jump closes the movie.

I do not commend the film's alternate ending per se. Staying together isn't inherently radical, but neither is deciding to break up. What is important about the alternate ending is Tom's sudden and miraculous recognition of what Jane had said; his willingness to be changed by love, which Tom fails to do in the film's theatrical ending.[31]

"Will you use the line you wrote on your Tumblr in your new book?" L asks. The line she is referring to is: "It was acted, which means it has the potential to be real."

On October 28, 2017, I wrote:

> *Broadcast News*' alternate ending offers a non-melancholic resolution to a predictable pattern of male behavior in the face of romantic relationships with strong, ambitious women. Not being able to handle a courageous, brilliant woman you claim to love is the equivalent of not being able to handle the world; not knowing how to live ethically. It makes a man—Tom—profoundly mediocre. Tom's mediocrity itself is the subject of the film. But at least the alternate ending exists. Even if it's not the one viewers ended up with 30 years ago, it is out there. It was dreamed up. It was acted, which means it has the potential to be real. Alternate ending Tom is not the Tom we get in the theatrical cut. It

31. *In The End of the Novel of Love* (1997), Vivian Gornick notes: "In a thousand novels of love-in-the-Western World, the progress of feeling between a woman of intelligence and a man of will is charted through a struggle that concludes itself when the woman at last melts into romantic longing and the deeper need for union . . . Just at this place where give is required, some flat cold inner remove seems to overtake the female protagonist. In the eyes of the world, she becomes opaque ('unnatural' she is called), but we, the privileged readers, know what is happening. The woman has taken a long look down the road of her future. What she sees repels. She cannot imagine herself in what lies ahead. Unable to 'imagine' herself, she now thinks she cannot act the part. She will no longer be able to make the motions."

is not the man Tom chooses to be at the end of the film. The man in the alternate ending is not the man that exceptional women normally end up with. For that we need an alternate ending. We get this alternate ending in the form of a special feature 30 years later. The theatrical cut gives us seven years, but it is not enough. One ending haunts the other ending. The possible haunts the actual. In the theatrical cut, Jane, being who she is, has to make the ethical decision: if Tom cannot be the man he should be, Jane cannot be the woman she is. And Jane must be the woman she is.

A miracle is always an alternate ending. In *Cinema* (2013), Alain Badiou, echoing Gilles Deleuze, writes: "You can film a miracle in cinema, and it may even be the case that cinema is the only art that has the potential to be miraculous." You can film a miracle by using light, he adds. Light being the magic element that eludes other art forms like painting and literature. Filmmaker Sidney Lumet writes that a camera "can make a miracle," but first "there is the light that exists even before it enters the lens." Literature can imagine the alternate ending and painting can abstract it, but cinema lets us actually *see* it. "Cinema can make the inner light of the visible appear. And at that moment, the visible itself becomes an event," writes Badiou.

Discussing the accidental green footage in *Call Me by Your Name*'s DVD commentary, Michael Stuhlbarg, who plays Elio's father, tells Timothée Chalamet, who plays Elio, "Film lets

32. In *Making Movies*, director Sidney Lumet observes that "Movies are the only art form that uses people to record something that is literally larger than life." In *Tokyo-ga*, shot in the spring of 1983, Wim Wenders notes that "each person knows for himself the extreme gap that often exists between personal experience and the depiction of that experience up there on the screen. We have learned to consider the vast difference separating cinema from life as so perfectly natural that

the light in and whatever happens becomes imprinted on the film."[32] Film actors do this too: make visible what is possible in human beings, letting the light in, and therefore function as contemporary miracles for their fans. Chalamet did it with Elio at the age of 22. The event, the "miracle," is watching him do it.[33] Watching him play the kind of person I stopped thinking existed even on film.

An actor's first task is to make themselves believe in who they are playing. In what they are saying. If they believe, we believe. It is because an actor can perform miracles on-screen that we believe they also want to do so in real life. Just as cinema gives us a reason to believe by restoring "the bond between human beings and world, in love or life," writes Deleuze, actors, by way of cinema, make being human—the bond between human and being—visible. Believable.

When I watch Elio wait all night for Oliver in *Call Me by Your Name*, I am reminded that love is important. That love takes a miracle. I do not believe that Elio and Oliver are in love. I believe that Elio is a person who is capable of love and because of this capacity, feels and acts accordingly, unlike Oliver. It is where we feel disappointment that we have the potential to still believe. Cinema, as Deleuze argues in *Time-Image*, does not film the world, it films *belief in the world*.[34] When Elio waits for Oliver, it is an example of belief. Watching Elio's act of faith restores my belief. This leads me back to the green footage in *Call Me by Your Name*—an accident, Luca Guadagnino tells us—and to Moyra Davey's passage on the loss of photographic latency in "Notes on Photography & Accident." While we gasp and give a start when we suddenly discover something true or real in a movie … It is a rarity in today's cinema to find such moments of truth." This could also work the other way around, as Robert Altman defined acting as "using up your own life." Arnaud Desplechin, whose 2019 police procedural *Roubaix, une Lumière (Roubaix, a Light)*, describes the "art of the actor" as an instrument that allows "reality to burn." In cinema, the actor is a metaphoric light (illumination) that burns up celluloid by making the visibility of reality possible. This idea of "burning"— an excess of light—conjures up Guadagnino's green celluloid burnout in *Call Me by Your Name* as well as Maria Falconetti's burning face in Carl Dreyer's *The Passion of Joan of Arc* (1928), which concludes the film. Lastly, discussing his performance in *Before the Rain* (1994), Yugoslav actor Rade Šerbedžija makes

James L. Brooks shelved the (latent) romantic possibility that lay dormant and unused in *Broadcast News* for 25 years, only sharing it with audiences after the film's Criterion release, Guadagnino took advantage of his "mistake" by revealing it.

In the audio introduction to *Broadcast News*' forgotten outtake, Brooks reveals that the alternate ending was improvised and shot due to what preview audiences felt was an "unfulfilling" conclusion, in which "nobody ends up with anybody." In the scene, which Brooks admits to watching for the first time since he shot it, the romantic leads both enter the frame, the inside of a taxicab. It is flooded with sunlight and grey-blue tones that match the their wardrobe, windows on every side. The two actors imbue the scene with something unscripted, unplanned; something extra that is different from the rest of the film. They are going to try to stay together. An attempt at a miracle.

the interesting distinction between theater acting and film acting when he says, "theater is acting; film is living."

33. In an interview, the French actor Grégoire Colin discusses film acting, the responsibilities of the camera, and not falling into the trap of acting as simulacra: "When you point the camera at someone, you have to want to film that person. It is a kind of loving gesture. Sometimes you get to know someone through his or her films and then the real encounter is disappointing. I hope it wasn't too disappointing with me. In my work I usually take my point of departure from movement: I envision how I might be in the given situation. It has to do with the interaction between a way of looking at things, of speaking and moving, so that the viewer can believe in the character. This subtle alchemy is absolutely necessary when trying to embody

What all these people are saying, is that film, unlike the digital, is the light that allows us to both reveal and to *see* what is possible. The miracle is to make visible what is possible so as to see what is possible. The miracle of seeing what is possible is always a call to ethics. For Badiou, the art of cinema is "not so much what we know as what we can know. To indicate what there could be, beyond what there is." [35] [36] For Godard, cinema is famously "truth 24 times a second."[37] For Deleuze, "The important thing is that the protagonist, or the spectator, or both, become visionary."

We should not be content with merely seeing what is possible, yet we are. We do a disservice to ourselves—and to others—by confining the miracle of cinema to cinema, and by reducing *making visible* what is possible (film) to seeing (the digital).[38] That is: to being truer for and with cinema than we are for and *because* of cinema. If you see a miracle, if you witness what is possible, a character." In his interview with Sam Jones in *Off Camera*, actor David Harbour talks about working with child actors in the Netflix series *Stranger Things* (2017). He describes the unselfconscious acting of Finn Wolfhard, who plays Mike, during the first season. Harbour observes that Wolfhard's prepubescent body moves in all kinds of unexpected and uncontrolled ways and is "just revealed" on camera. A child actor—versus an adult actor—"just kind of does it." In a 2016 interview

it is a call to change, restoring the link between perception (what we see) and practice (what we do about what we see). By reminding me of the line I wrote about miracles, L is also telling me something I have forgotten: *you are still capable of believing.*[39]

with Build, Harbour told Ricky Camilleri, "The thing about acting is we make choices, but ultimately we can't hide ourselves. Like, ultimately you reveal yourself as a human being when you act." This echoes David Fincher's description of Mark Ruffalo's acting in *Zodiac*, "He's such a person."

34. John Cassavetes noted the following about his movie, *Minnie and Moskowitz* (1971): "To understand the story of *Minnie and Moskowitz* and the relationship of the title characters through their fights, arguments, pounding on doors, the torture, the pain, the screaming and the eventual marriage, it is essential for the audience to take itself back to when it cared." In other words, we once went to the movies in order to care. Bresson told *Opera* something similar in 1951: "As for my film, certainly don't look for it to explain anything; ask only that it

return you to your inner child." Filmmaker Arnaud Desplechin has also expressed this view in the Criterion documentary, *Arnaud's Tale* (2008): "When I'm in a theater looking at the screen, I can see how wide reality is, and this is the pure truth. That's why I believe much more in films rather than real life."

35. bell hooks has often stated that the aim of art should be to document what could be, not simply what is. To explore the possible versus the actual. This is not to be confused with fantasy.

36. Alain Badiou, *Cinema*, Polity Press, 2013

37. Godard: "If the invisible were visible, what might we see?" (*Scénario du film "Passion,"* 1982)

38. In the case of *Broadcast News*, the miracle of seeing what is possible in cinema is both accessed and retrieved through the digital. Our compulsive use of the smartphone at music concerts might explain how we have replaced experiencing what is possible with pure seeing. For Deleuze, "the task of *believing* and *producing belief* in the world," belongs to the theology of cinema. As it stands, cinema is—or was—the place we went to in order to dream up alternatives—to care as Cassavetes instructs; to see what we do not believe exists outside of cinema, or do not know how to see outside of cinema. We have failed to foster links not just between images, writes Deleuze, but between images and life; a precious link that can restore our faith in the world. In *How to Grow Old*, Cicero reminds us in 44 BC: "...do not stop believing even if you will see nothing."

39. In an email on December 7, 2020, an astrologer friend, who had rewatched *Broadcast News* in 2020, happily informed me: "Did you know Holly Hunter and William Hurt have the same birthday?!"

I miss old skyscrapers.

Maybe there won't even be a
building standing anymore

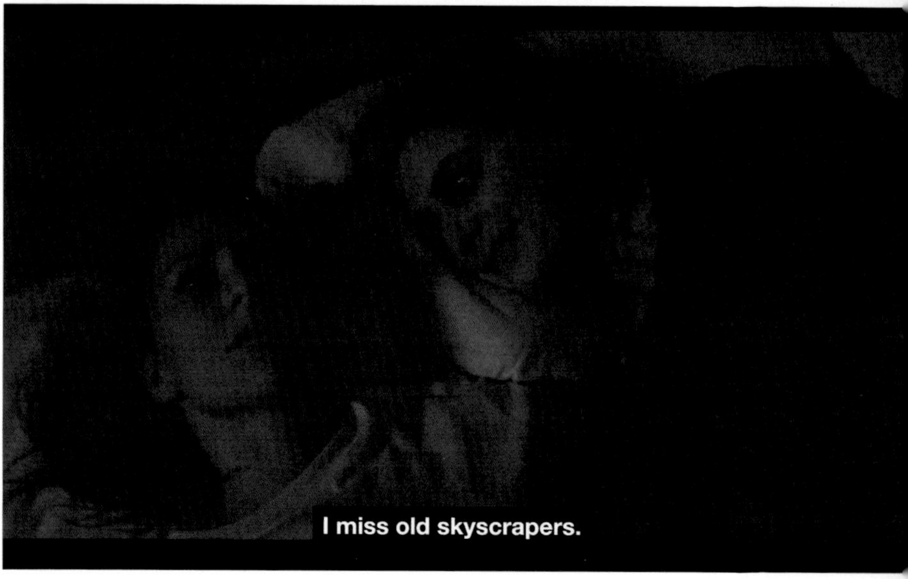

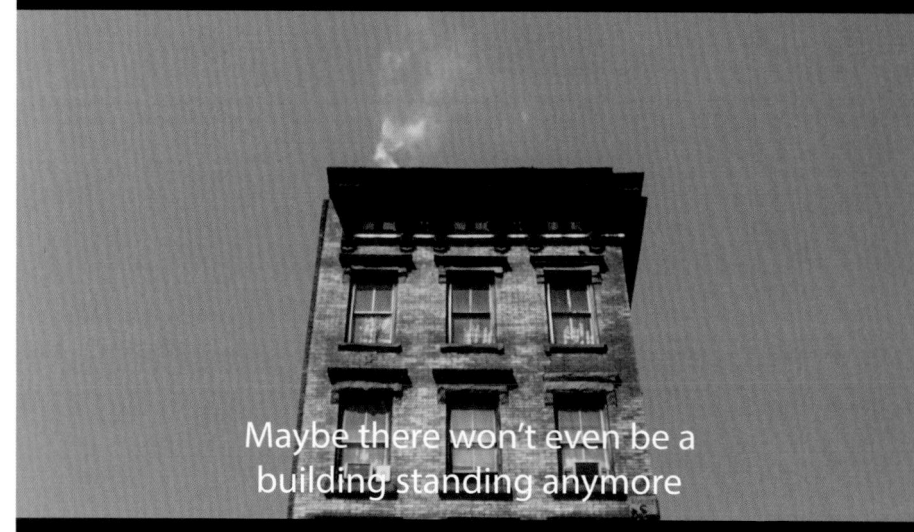

TIME TELLS

PART I:
EARLY BREAKS

"I months later saw the clock image which I interpreted as meaning this will take time."
—Hannah Weiner, *The Fast*

In the movies the time-jump serves as a numerical shorthand for a fated intermission. The time-jump uses the language of the calendar as well as *mise-en-scène* to log what happens between acts. As a screen graphic of return (*ritorno*), time is revealed as the unknowable becoming knowable, the impossible becoming possible.

Many early movies were screened with intermissions in the form of *entr'actes*—a piece of live or recorded music performed between the first and second half of a movie. An entr'acte, or intermezzo in Italian, is also an interval between the wrong time and the right time. Movie intermissions were initially a product of projection technology. 35 mm films were printed on multiple spools. This required projectionists to cue up movies on two different projectors, working diligently, as Adrian Bernhard writes in *The Atlantic*, "to get these cues and timings right." Intermissions gave projectionists the time to do this. Even after the multiple reel system was upgraded to multiple projectors in the

1970s, making intermissions unnecessary, interludes between acts offered spectators a break, encouraging them to use concession stands, particularly at American drive-ins (In 1957, an animated musical advertisement was introduced before the main feature or during intermission. It sang: "Let's all go to the lobby to get ourselves a snack."). In their original theatrical releases, movies like *Gone with the Wind* (1939), *East of Eden* (1955), *Lawrence of Arabia* (1962), *The Godfather* (1972), and *Gandhi* (1982) all employed the intermission as narrative structure.[40] The live intermission was built into the recorded movie. Nondiegetic suspension became diegetic. Divided into two parts, epic movies like *Gone with the Wind* (4 min., 4 sec. interlude), *Lawrence of Arabia* (1 min., 23 sec. interlude), and *Ghandi* (3 min. interlude) were preceded by musical interludes and title cards. The time-jump, which eventually took the form of a time and date, was initially expressed only by the word "Intermission."

While the intermission imposes a break in real time, splitting the movie screening into two parts, the time-jump declares a diegetic lapse by noting it on screen. After the built-in movie intermission was phased out of the epic film, timestamps and time-jumps became more common, fusing live music and live intermissions as well as recorded music and montage. A trope as well as a narrative device, the time-jump is an electronically generated caption that is superimposed on a television or movie screen to note the unseen time that has elapsed (usually between estranged lovers) in a diegetic narrative. The caption, termed "chiron" in 1971, and

40. The 1982 bio-epic *Gandhi* officially phased the intermission out of Western mainstream cinema. Whereas in other parts of the world, such as "India's thriving Bollywood," writes Nathan Hartman, "it wasn't until 2011's *Mumbai Diaries* that a film was even released there without one." ("What Happened to the Movie Intermission?: Let's All Go Back to the Lobby," 2014, *The Outtake*).

later "chyron," was originally derived from a graphics manufacturing machine called Chyron. Like the intermission, the time-jump both preserves time and corrects it.

In analog cinema, "information always takes up physical space," writes Peter Suderman. With digital filmmaking and projection, "there's more variety in the ways movies are shot and projected than ever before, and more choices for both filmmakers and moviegoers. And that can lead to confusion." The noncommittal "profusion of formats" has made the intermission, along with the time-jump, largely meaningless. If the analog movie viewer used their movie break to visit bathrooms and concession stands, the digital spectator requires a break from time itself. "Whether viewers find the experience of sitting through an overture enriching or torturous," Bernhard concludes, "is hard to say. It's likely that many never take the time to find out." Reintroducing intermissions to today's extra-long digital features, flips the source of distraction. By checking their smartphone and social media during a break instead of during a screening, the digital-age viewer splits their attention rather than a movie's running time.

ENTR'ACTE

INTERMISSION

Length came to define mid-2000s cinema. According to *Business Insider*, movies in 2012 were 1.2 times longer than movies in 1992. Post-millennial epics like *Inherent Vice* (2014), *Interstellar* (2014), *Exodus: Gods and Kings* (2014), *Blade Runner 2049* (2017), *Once Upon a Time in Hollywood* (2019), *Uncut Gems* (2019), and *The Irishman* (2019), all approach or breach a three-hour running time. A. O. Scott wrote that both *Once Upon a Time* and *The Irishman* "tackle the mysteries of time" despite *The Irishman*'s famous deep-fake approach to aging. Given that blockbusters today "are, on average, longer than they were just 20 years ago," many critics bemoan expanding length while others propose a reinstatement of movie intermissions as a possible solution:

> "*Vulture* has taken to offering guides for would-be audiences on the best moments to take much needed bathroom breaks during particularly long movies... If the film reaches or exceeds 2½ hours in length, give us a break! Bring back the intermission."[41]

If attention spans are getting shorter, and programmed distraction has become our primary mode of viewing,[42] then why are the running times of Hollywood movies increasing? Does a break in the middle of a long movie extend or shorten a film?

41. Aisha Harris, *Slate*, 2014

42. In *Present Shock*, Douglas Rushkoff describes this as "the *kairos* we're being distracted from."

OVERTURE

INTERMISSION

ENTR' ACTE

René Clair's 1924 27-minute Dadaist short, *En'tracte*, is organized into two parts. A "little" overture, about 90 seconds long (time indications are not precise as film and music techniques at the time of the premiere did not allow for accurate timing), features the experimental French composer Eric Satie and avant-garde multimedia artist Francis Picabia firing a cannon (aimed at the viewer) from the rooftop of a Paris building. The film premiered as an *en'tracte* for "Relâche," performed by Ballets Suédois and written by Picabia. It was performed at the Théâtre des Champs-Elyseés in Paris. When the show was cancelled, Picabia, who conceived of the ballet as a Dadaist practical joke, commissioned Clair to create a "cinematographic en'tracte" to be shown during the ballet's intermission.

In this case, *En'tracte* is the world before cinema and after cinema. In Clair's highly imaginative exercise, the clockwork universe splits reality into two acts. One world moves at a normal speed, the other—the industrialized world; the camera world—is sped up, slowed down, compressed all at the same time. Cinema, as Clair's film—an example of L'INSTANTANÉISME, which believes, as its manifesto states, "ONLY IN PERPETUAL MOTION"—demonstrates, reinvents time by allowing us to go forward and backward simultaneously. Clair's experimentation with the tempo of different kinds of mechanical and nonmechanical movement, which he layers and superimposes, makes time a camera's plaything. The train, locomotive, roller-coaster, and bicycle are all fast. But cinema is faster. At the end of *En'tracte*, a magician bursts out of a coffin, through the "FIN" screen title, tearing the words "FIN" apart, only to then rewind and restitch the title back together. Cinema here is a magic wand that can make things appear and disappear. It turns an ending back into a beginning.

Cinema is an en'tracte because it alters both the future and the past. And while movies may be illusion-making machines that "value the instant," as *instantaneism* declared, they also invented new spatial and temporal relations, altering the course of human destiny. Time is rearranged.

INTERMISSION

INTERMISSION

Unlike the time montage, which speeds up time by crunching it visually or musically, the time-jump is a temporal non-structure or ellipsis; an omission of the *movement* of time in the form of a static time-*image*. It is time appearing *as itself*—not as *movement-image* but as a destinal *time-image* of what is not shown or seen in the diegetic story. An example of what Gilles Deleuze describes in *Cinema 2* as "situations and spaces we no longer know how to describe," the time-jump morphs into a time-image because it represents the delay and suspension we no longer know how to experience or emotionally withstand. In the case of love, it also records a situation we no longer know how to be in. Douglas Rushkoff refers to this ontological situation as the "spaces between the ticks." Clarice Lispector wrote, "The tick tock is it." In *Lightning Over Water*, Wim Wenders' 1979 documentary on the great Nicholas Ray, Ray (who was terminally ill with cancer by this point), curses his Mickey Mouse clock when it wakes him in his Soho loft. He refuses to shut it off. "Hey!" Ray pleads over and over, tucking the toy clock under his blanket to muffle it. Eventually he gives up and gets out of bed, obeying the alarm's command. "Ticker" is also an idiom for heart. In his essay, *L'Intrus*, Jean-Luc Nancy describes this strange liminality, the spaces between the ticks, as "the sensation of passing over a bridge, while still remaining on it." Time is the bridge. We are the ones crossing it. Together the link in the break is preserved. Time contains all its moving parts, which is to say, it contains *us* in the moving parts of time. While the invention of the calendar produced the clockwork universe—an industrialized metaphor for being—the digital economy produces an uncountable algorithm, where time neither *passes* nor *jumps*. Neither ticks nor tocks. No longer existential or descriptive, digital time is always caught in the predatory Now.

Programmed time—time in advance—tells us what to do and how to do it, but nothing about when or why.[43] The time-jump is intimately bound with and contingent upon *kairos*, but what is *kairos* when time is *code*?

43. In *The Bluest Eye*, Toni Morrison concludes: "But since why is difficult to handle, one must take refuge in how."

Rushkoff:

> Our analog technologies anchored us temporally in ways our digital ones don't. In a book or a scroll, the past is on our left, and the future is on our right. We know where we are in linear time by our position in the paper. While the book with its discrete pages is a bit more sequential than the scroll, both are entirely more oriented in time than the computer screen. Whichever program's window we may open at the moment is the digital version of no, without context or placement in the timeline.

PART II:
TIME IS OVER

"Whatever used to tell the time
Is mute and deaf and blind."
—Nietzsche, *The Gay Science*

In *Beyond Good and Evil*, Friedrich Nietzsche writes that the problem of dormancy and expectancy (waiting), the postponement or skirting of "the right time," is resolved by acting at the right time for what he calls the "eternal return."[44] That is, in a manner that permits something that *could* happen to *happen*. This call is often heard but ignored. For Nietzsche, the ability to act comes from a call that is not merely *heard*, but correctly and opportunely *seized*. While Deleuze correlates the shift from time-movement to time-image with post-war life in Europe (what Franco Berardi has termed "the slow cancellation of future," in which "the subordination of time to movement was reversed," and where "time ceases to be the measurement of normal movement, increasingly appearing for itself and creating paradoxical movements"), Rushkoff, who is writing at a much later date in 2013, equates present shock with narrative collapse and the loss of duration. "Present shock," a term Rushkoff borrows from Alvin Toffler's 1965 essay, "The Future as a Way of Life," in which Toffler introduces the concept of "future shock," forces us to live "outside what we have always thought of as time." Rushkoff's

44. As I wrote in *Love Dog* (2013), the question of when is the right time to act is central to Shakespeare's *Hamlet*.

analysis of the shift from movement-time to time-image can be applied to Nicolas Winding Refn's driver in *Drive* (2011). In the movie, a post-millennial male drifter is constantly moving but his pastiche future is always already behind him. *Drive*'s hero sports a vintage wristwatch, masking the film's digiphrenic outlook by wearing a fetishized past (his retro-chic clothes also evoke the idea of *wearing* time).[45]

Refn's *Drive* is an example of the presentist time code. Its getaway driver (Ryan Gosling) is noncommittal, famously giving the thieves he chauffeurs five-minute windows before he abandons them. Every heist is prepped with the same disclaimer:

> "You give me a time and a place, I give you a five-minute window. Anything happens in that five minutes, and I'm yours. No matter what. Anything happens the minute either side of that, and you're on your own."

Instead of using a digital timer to track his five-minute windows, the driver uses his mechanical wristwatch—a more imprecise, and therefore more subjective, system of time; a time that can easily be *miscalculated* if one stops looking at the clock; if one stops *counting* (especially in a dark car late at night). The romantic induction "I'm yours" sounds vaguely like a love speech. The driver's rehearsed and rehashed soliloquy is meant to symbolize heroism, dependability, and loyalty, but instead presents the heroism of white post-millennial heteromasculinity as a sound-bite-ontology. The driver will echo the same

[45]. In the 1988 movie *Criminal Law*, Gary Oldman's character, Ben Chase, uses a flashlight to read the time on his analog wristwatch. Without the flashlight, he literally cannot see the time. It is too dark in his car.

five-minute mantra when he meets love interest, Irene (Carey Mulligan), propositioning her with, "You got five minutes?"

The present the driver offers his criminal clients may be all-inclusive, but anything beyond the short *forever* does not exist. The strict, conditional contract of the driver's minutes-long devotion exists in tandem with the precarity and transience of social bonds under 24/7 technocapitalism. Unlike Frank (James Caan), the working class criminal in *Thief* (1981), who actively mourns the years he's lost in prison—"I'm gonna put it back together"—Gosling's driver, a hipster in his twenties, is never off his monetized watch. He charges for the minute before and the minute after. The urban sprawl of twenty-first century Los Angeles ("There's 100,000 streets in the city"), a blend of movies, genres, time periods, and styles, is nevertheless a 24/7 wasteland. There is, as the driver tells us, nothing on the other side of the stipulated window of digital time, only the brief minutes in between. While Frank, a top-line jewel thief, is pressed for time due to countless years (eleven) lost in prison, the young moody driver has no time to spare, pre-programming every minute in advance. Frank's, "You don't count months and years. You don't do time that way. You gotta forget time," turns into the driver's, "You give me a time and a place. I give you a five-minute window." Frank has run out of time and therefore cherishes every minute.[46] The driver, a violent melancholic who anticipates and bills for time losses in advance, reminds people when their time is up *ahead* of time. Despite all the driving, *Drive*'s emphasis on the "pure state of time," on an absence of actual movement, produces what Deleuze refers to as a false movement and what Rushkoff calls present shock.[47]

46. As stated in *Manhunter*, *Miami Vice*, and *Heat*, for Michael Mann "Time is luck."

47. In an interview for Radio-télévision française in 1950, Robert Bresson tells Pierre Desgraupes: "… what we have understood so far as 'motion,' the kind of motion, or movement, we currently seek in films, is nothing more than restlessness."

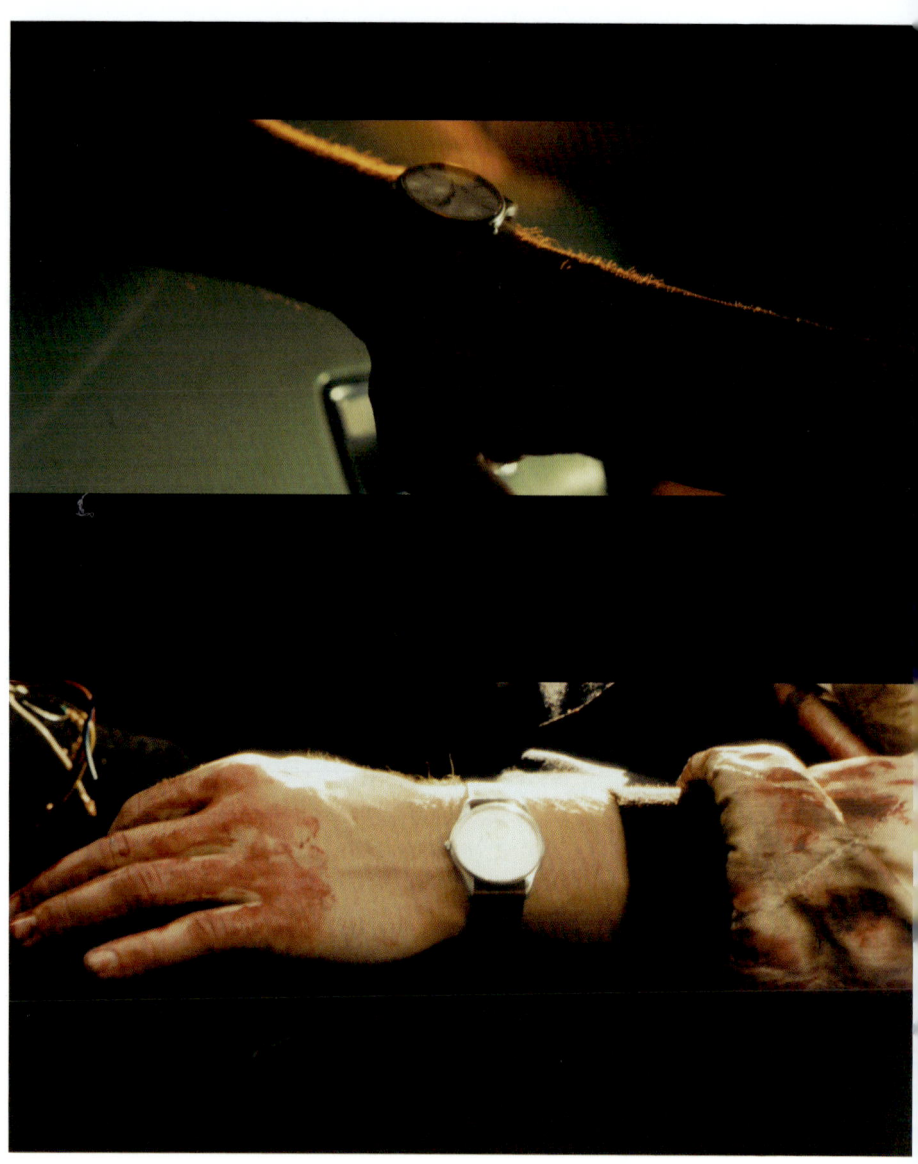

In cinema, unlike life, one rarely waits in vain. Cinema itself is in part a response to the problem of not "seizing chance by its forelock" (Nietzsche). The cinematic time-jump is always tracking an expectancy—something that is pending. Coming. Something that must be acted for when it arrives. Returns. Time is not for *no* thing but rather for *some* thing. In present shock, ontological clocks are rewired and scrambled. Waiting becomes anachronistic, a lost phenomenology.[48] Relationships to and with time are turned into technologies of relationship. The driver's analog wristwatch, along with Refn's close-ups of it, is merely an aestheticization of time rather than any real engagement with it.

In *24/7: Late Capitalism and the Ends of Sleep*, Jonathan Crary examines late capitalism's drive to reimagine the planet "as a nonstop work site." No longer part of the clockwork universe, or the schedule universe, "24/7 steadily undermines distinctions between day and night, between light and dark, and between action and repose . . . It is a zone of insensibility, of amnesia, of what defeats the possibility of experience." A 24/7 life is a life that is predicated on a consumptive wakefulness. How, asks Crary, paraphrasing Maurice Blanchot, do we orient ourselves ontologically and *expectantly* in a 24/7 world—"a time of indifference"? If time is monetized and preprogrammed, unmarked by breaks or stops, how is it *lived*? How is it *felt*? "There's this sense in digital time that every moment is like every other moment," Rushkoff stated during a talk at New York's McNally Jackson bookstore in 2013. "That time is somehow generic. 3:02 might as well be 3:03 might as well be 3:04."[49]

48. "It Is What It Is," a song by millennial singer Dev Hynes of Blood Orange, is a musical and lyrical leitmotif in Luca Guadagnino's 2020 HBO series *We Are Who We Are*. Both the song and the series are exemplar non-committal titles indicative of the post-millennial era. The lyrical refrain of "It Is What It Is," "No one's waiting for you anyway, so don't be stressed out" demonstrates a clear break with the romantic waiting phenomenology the time-jump once represented. "No one's waiting for you" is meant to be a comforting anti-ontology for post-millennials. In the impassioned "Praying for Time" (1990), George Michael puts it beautifully and succinctly, "Maybe we should all be praying for time." Hynes and Guadagnino's contemporary teens seem to advocate for the opposite.

49. Douglas Rushkoff, *Present Shock: When Everything Happens Now*, Current, 2013

from 5:00 to 6:30 p.m.

Creating insomniac conditions out of life is one way to induce an anti-ontological imperative in which there is no time or reason to wait for anything. Netflix has even proudly stated that its only competitor is sleep. Though sleep cannot be eliminated, Crary notes, it can be wrecked, delayed, and made laborious. Life becomes insomniac and incoherent. In *Being & Neonness*, Luis de Miranda reflects on the history of neon, which, he argues, is also the history of technocapitalism: "In the twentieth century, controlling light meant controlling society through consumption, and this is still true today through the light of our computer or phone screen. Electrical lightning sold stuff."

As an endocrine disruptor, the blue screen of smart devices is the twenty-first century's equivalent of neon. A continuous network of light, the blue glow of our home monitors and smartphones is—like neon—the corporatization of night, cortisol, and time. As the light that never goes off, blue screens transactionalize our dreams or hijack them completely. Of course, sleep is not the same thing as rest. Sleep, as Freud tells us, is also work.

While a consumer dictatorship thrives on a nonstop cycle of appearance and disappearance, upload and download, consumption and disposal, the cinematic time-jump is a fated notation of pause and return; an embodied destinal phenomenology made possible by a carefully timed suspension and expectancy, sequence and recurrence. The 24/7 timeframe, however, is "unrelieved wakefulness,"[50] devoid of temporal alternatives or variability. Disembodied 24/7 time has no past and no future. "24/7 announces a time without time,"[51] closing any opening for the quantum-leap of a fated return.[52]

50. Jonathan Crary, *24/7: Late Capitalism and the Ends of Sleep*, p. 19

51. Jonathan Crary, *24/7: Late Capitalism and the Ends of Sleep*, p. 29

52. Echoing Crary, in the podcast *Team Human*, Rushkoff states that "digital technology is used to optimize human beings for the marketplace, whether as labor or as consumers, and that means total interchangeability." One person can be traded for another, which is one reason the time-jump does not work in the digital Now of constant replication. In "Netflix and Chills: On Digital Distraction During the Global Quarantine," Dominic Pettman writes, "Modernity, for [Heidegger], represented nothing more or less than 'the forgetting of Being,' thanks to the inoculating efficiency of modern technologies, automated habits, alienating impulses, and existential disavowals."

10 Years Later

WHAT DID HE DO IN THE INTERVAL?

PART III:
TIME OUT

". . . is there a historian of the promise?"
—Jacques Derrida, *Archive Fever: An Freudian Impression*

In 2014, Fox News aired a segment on the structural development of time-jumps in post-millennial television programs like *How I Met My Mother* (2005) and *Breaking Bad* (2008). Most viewers confessed they were baffled and "couldn't follow" time-jumps. And yet, time-jumps are a common device, especially in the science fiction and romantic comedy genres, in which lovers struggle to sync in time and ill-fated encounters frequently drive plot. Others insisted time-jumps only made sense if they're "done well." When I first googled "time-jumps" it was 2014, and apart from an Urban Dictionary entry, there were no articles online. The space the search opened as a field of inquiry was like the fated lacuna the time-jump represents.

Urban Dictionary described the time-jump as:

> A time-jump is a period of time during which an event is not seen but is mentioned or referred to. This happens constantly in movies and soap operas.

On TV and VHS releases, overtures, interludes, and titles were often edited out because they literally take up too much time. In the case of syndicated television, commercials take precedence as corporate intermissions. Often these title cards can only be found in restored DVD versions, but not always. In the looped TBS broadcasts of the 2001 rom-com *Serendipity*, the two opening time-jumps that organize the movie—"A few years ago" and "A few years later"—were both cut.

A few years ago

A few years later

The first few times I watched *Serendipity* on television, I viewed it without the two time-jumps that structure the film. Without them, the movie's star-crossed lovers plot makes little sense. The narrative seems arbitrary and confusing. Why is their hair longer now? Why are they suddenly engaged to other people? Why do they live in different cities? Without the time-jumps, there is nothing to indicate that time has passed—*jumped*. That time has become a problem that must be attended to and fixed.

In *Broadcast News*, the time-jump is put into crisis as a romantic trope and narrative device. However, rather than resolve romantic crisis through a fated intermission, the time-jump merely *clocks* the realization of romantic irreconcilability and freezes it. Time is not the problem, mismatched ethics are—a problem time cannot rectify for Tom and Jane. In *Broadcast News*, the time-jump underscores this logistical gap, it does not close it.[53] Time is deadlocked. The incompatible lovers could not be together then and they won't be together "seven years later." Time passes but the problem is not time. The reason for Jane's breakup with Tom endures across time as what cannot be amended. The "wrong time" is actually the wrong person who nevertheless will always recall something that felt fated and right. The theatrical ending of *Broadcast News* jarringly reverses the screwball comedy paradigm, in which romantic happiness consists of two people, "paired by chance and against their wishes," learning to be together.[54]

53. As I have noted in "Alternate Endings," a 25-year-old unreleased alternate ending corrects what the movie's 7-year time-jump could not. The digital supplement replaces the taxonomy of the diegetic time-jump. In *The Act of Seeing*, Wim Wenders dismisses *Broadcast News*' time-jump ending—7 years later—as a "fake ending tacked onto *Broadcast News* that takes the whole thing back," ignoring the gendered implications of the passage of time for women like Jane. I have already explained what I mean by "women like Jane," as well as women like Katie Morosky from *The Way We Were*. What the 7 years later time-jump coda makes clear is precisely the consequence of the decision Jane makes when she chooses ethics over pseudo-love, as Erich Fromm termed it. While the two male leads in *Broadcast News* both end up with wives, children,

and careers, Jane only ends up with a career. The decision she makes to leave Tom becomes a permanent cross to bear. While everyone else's lives go on, the time-jump makes Jane's decision something irreversible. It would be more accurate to say that *Broadcast News* has three endings: the ending of Jane in the taxi after she leaves Tom at the airport, the ending after the time-jump, and the deleted ending we see thirty years later. It is interesting, however, that Wenders uses a temporal analogy to discredit the ending he doesn't like—"takes the whole thing back." Takes it back where, we might ask? While *Broadcast News*' time-jump careens us into the future, Wenders claims it sets us back.

54 Scott Spencer, *A Ship Made of Paper*, HarperCollins, 2003

In *Broadcast News*' penultimate scene, Jane holds two fingers against her forehead. This hand gesture—both a symbol for loser upside down and a gun pointed at her own head—represents a crossroads and a cross to bear. A fork in the road of her life. Did Jane make the right decision? Should she go back? What awaits her now? She is marking herself. Signing how it feels. Her eyes close. Time jumps.

The realization is unbearable: Jane cannot and will not be with Tom. A taxi drives her away; into the future of her decision; into the time-jump of seven years later.

Released in 1987, *Broadcast News* voids the time-jump of its destinal phenomenology, reducing it to a temporal anachronism for aborted *fin de siècle* movie romances. For how can time—and the waiting and expectancy that comes with it—be the answer, if, as Crary points out, time has become not simply, "a homogenous and unvariegated time, but rather ... a disabled and derelict diachrony ... there are differentiated temporalities, but the range and depth of distinctions between them diminishes, and an unimpeded substitutability between times becomes normalized"? In *Broadcast News*, the distinction between now and then—between seven years earlier and seven years later—is simply a general sense of loss. The time-jump is reduced to an irrelevant and defunct index that leads nowhere.

"Human beings do not meet the way two lines intersect at some precise point on a grid," writes Stephen Kern in *The Culture of Love: Victorians to Moderns*. "They meet one another in a specific place that is unlike any other and invested with meaning." This "specific place" is actually a specific time. The smartphone is simultaneously unspecific (you can be anywhere, at any time) and a precise point on the grid (geographical locations are tracked).

The time-jump describes what is not shown. It is a fated sum. When a time-jump appears on-screen, the viewer should try to imagine not simply what happened later, but the years in between.[55] The knowledge one accumulates

55. "...suffering alone reveals the total significance of the beloved object," writes Georges Bataille in *Death and Sensuality*, 1969.

through waiting. The years spent in pain. The existential calendar rather than the programmed literalism of the digiphrenic network. These are counted years. Lived years. Felt years. Hidden years. These are even lost years. These are the years since. The years after. The years *between*. We cannot see these years because cinema is not durational (slow), it is compressive. It is timed for a reunion. It is destinal. It is a phenomenology of cutting and stitching. The time that we do not see is as important as the time we do see. We know how long these years have been by the summative number, which is not only a notation of separation, of the time spent *away* from something or someone, but an affective tally, what the historian Jacques Le Goff calls the "psychologizing of duration." The time-jump tells us what and who has been missing, and for how long. The appearance of the time-jump on-screen always comes as a surprise because in the traditional linear story, "emotional experience is entirely bound up in time," writes Rushkoff. The time-jump is a sign that there may now be another chance.[56] The passage of time is the vehicle for that chance, which is also called *timing* (*kairos*). Time returns.

If it were not for time. Because of time. Maybe this time.[57]

In the post-narrative streaming era, we consume time all at once, without pause. Without appointments. Without timed breaks. Without metaphysical timetables. Without cause and effect. In *Broadcast News*, the time-jump tells us: time did not attend to this wound. Time froze it and left it there.

56. In 1979, Jean-Luc Godard told Marguerite Duras: "I just tell myself that the purpose of a film or a book is simply to say, 'it could not be over,' as if you could rewind or fast-forward, like on a tape recorder." Godard repeats these words a year later on the soundtrack of his film *Every Man for Himself* (1980).

57. After a four-year time-jump flashes on screen in the 2016 British crime series, *The Night Manager*, the titular hero opens up a book where he has stashed the name of a mysterious intelligence agency operative. The night manager has left Cairo for Switzerland after his lover is murdered. Significantly, this phone number is lodged within the pages of *The Letters of T. E. Lawrence* during part four—*The Years of Hide and Seek.*

2 HOURS

Nine Years.

Is 50 years a long time?

The years went by for me too

Temporal.

But how can I describe frozen time?

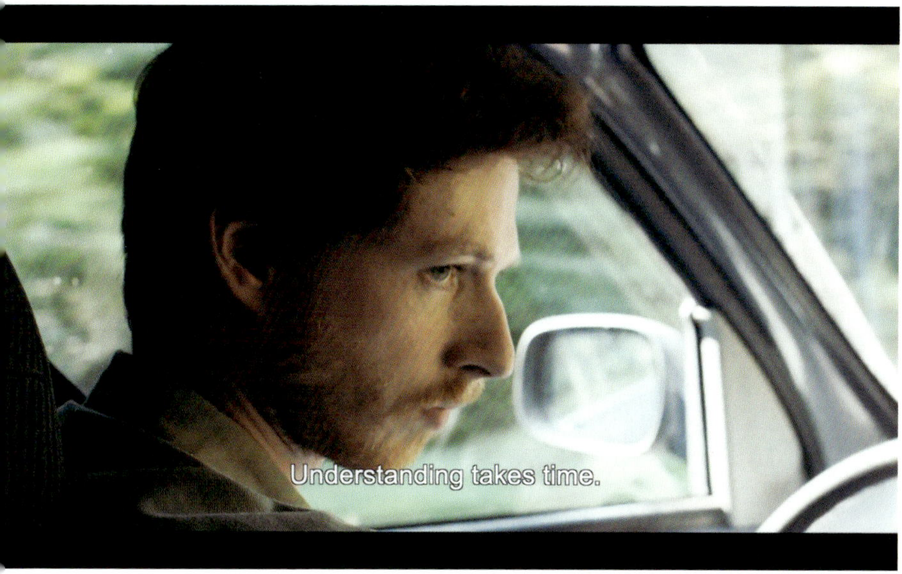
Understanding takes time.

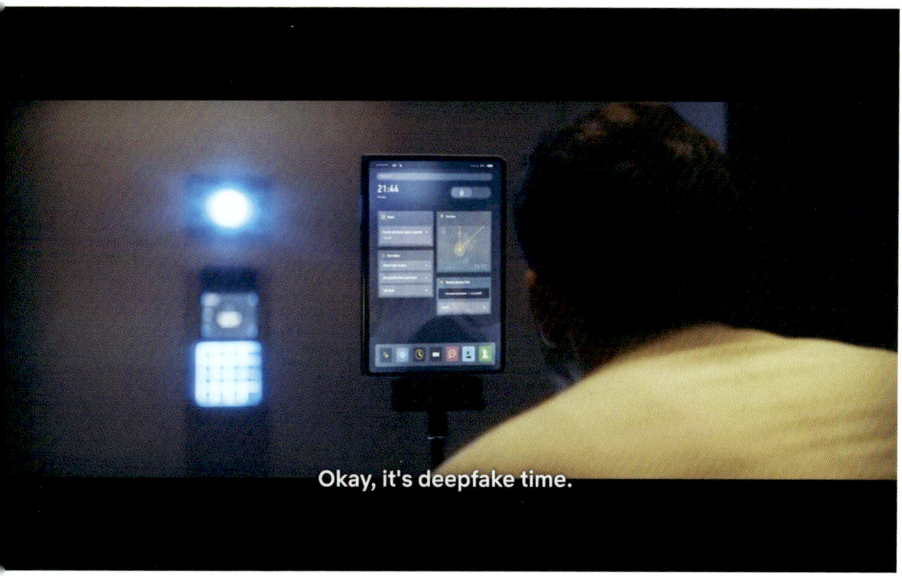
21:44
Okay, it's deepfake time.

Five years later.

DIX ANS APRÈS (1972)

Ten years later...

In a 1980 television appearance on the Dick Cavett show, Jean-Luc Godard described his filmmaking by fusing Deleuze's movement-time with time-image.[58] "Time is the space between people," Godard told Cavett, and "movies are the train, not the station."[59] In his melancholic train analogy, which I first took to mean the modern location where lovers both separate and reunite (*Brief Encounter* and *Before Sunrise* being two famous examples; Wim Wenders' *Wrong Move* also has a poignant train sequence), and later realize is Godard's reference to the birth of cinema itself—the Lumière Brother's *The Arrival of a Train at La Ciotat Station*—Godard claims he has given up on "waiting" for cinema, which he personifies. "It is because of the camera that we can talk to each other," he tells a perplexed Cavett.[60] If it is because of the camera that we can talk to each other, much of twentieth century cinema posits that it was because of the train that we could love each other—rencounter each other, go back to each other.

Time-jump.

58. Jean-Luc Godard, *The Dick Cavett Show*, 1980. A line from Marguerite Duras' 1983 film *Roman Dialogue* also comes to mind here: "Often, it will be unbearable. When, at night, he will awaken, knowing that she's still there, for a brief time, what separates them from the vessel of arrival."

59. In *Tokyo-ga* (1985), Wim Wenders makes this touching remark: "The trains, the trains, all the trains in [Yasujiro] Ozu's films. Not a single film in which there isn't at least one train." Claire Denis, on the other hand, sees the train in terms of immobility and passivity. But unlike a plane, she says, "You see the movement of the train."

60. Describing a 2001 exhibition that Dominique Païni organized in Montreal and Paris where "each [object] encapsulates a certain Hitchcock movie," Laura Mulvey writes, "Looking at

the Païni display, even through tears, it was impossible not to remember that nothing looks better than when it was made from light." In 1962, Alfred Hitchcock told François Truffaut that there is no such thing as a face without the light of cinema. Was this also true of the portrait in painting?

In the case of Godard's conversation with Cavett, the camera in the televised studio setting is the reason we can see—and can continue to see, via YouTube—Dick Cavett and Godard discuss cinema. As a form of transportation, cinema, Godard explains, is "the time you need to get to someone else." "That's what film is for," Hitchcock told Truffaut, "to either contract time or extend it. Whatever you wish." Time is a space that must be passed through and endured. The time-jump's time count is the ontological heading that tells us how long two characters have been apart before they are reunited. As a proxy for love, cinema facilitates an amorous reunion just as the train facilitates geographical movement—motion. Under this supposition, cinema operates under a wishful premise: second chances, reunions, returns, do-overs. The whatever you wish is a correction of time (the subjunctive mood). But there are moments, Hitchcock adds, "when you have to stop time."

"How many hours do you think he's been sitting there?" Michael Stuhlbarg asks Timothée Chalamet on the commentary track for *Call Me by Your Name*. Stuhlbarg is referring to the scene in which Elio—lovesick—spends the entire night waiting for Oliver to come home. Stuhlbarg acts as though Chalamet had really waited; as though Elio and Oliver were real; as though Chalamet were actually Elio. In the scene, there is nothing to distract Elio from his object of desire. No smartphone to sublimate his longing. No emotional technology on the scene. In the digital universe, writes Rushkoff, "We each have our own computer or device onto which we install our choice of software, and then use or respond to it individually." Time is hoarded, individuated. There is no "background for the foreground," and timelines are no longer synchronous. In both the clockwork universe and the time-jump universe, time must be passed through and shared, for something worthwhile is waiting on the other side.

In movies, the time-jump often functions as a mysterious time-out; a reset in the form of time having finally yielded after deadlock. Because timing in love is thought to be both an impediment and the panacea, time is cut and circumvented on-screen. While we may not know what makes people ready for something, in cinema a recalibration of time was almost always the answer. But how do we know what time is for now? "This 'after,'" writes Derrida, "which determines a sequence, a consequence, or a persecution, is not in time, nor is it temporal: it is the very genesis of time." While most mainstream films adhere to a time frame that is monetarily budgeted, it is not the movement of time that is inexpressible on-screen, it is the mysterious duration and timeline of love itself.

The Way We Were also uses time-lapses to explore the trials of modern love. In the retroactive 1973 saga, which begins in the 1930s and ends in the 1950s, the time-jump does not take the form of a specific number of days or years. Instead, the movie uses two dissolves to book-end and compress an unspecified amount of time. The first time-lapse opens the film, the second closes it. The present and the future are cut to converge upon the two leads' faces. Hers and his.

When Katie Morosky (Barbra Streisand) first encounters Hubbell Gardner (Robert Redford) years after they've gone their separate ways at the beginning of *The Way We Were*, he is casually sleeping on a barstool in a rowdy New York night club just before the end of World War II. He is now a naval officer in the South Pacific; she works at radio station. Many years have gone by since Katie and Hubbell first met at college, where he was a popular jock and she was a studious, working-class Marxist Jew. The film begins in a flashback that doubles as a prologue.[61] In a present that is a memory. Time jumps backwards to when the two collegiates met. The tragedy of *The Way We Were* is its temporal deadlock of sexual politics, which fated reunions and time-lapses fail to mend.[62] Hubbell's lifeless masculinity—he is both literally and metaphorically asleep—is a sexual anachronism that ensnares Katie for more than twenty years.

Reaching back into the past, Katie's hand is spectral, supernatural, as it brushes Hubbell's golden hair from his brow. It is an act of sorcery. Time is a spell. Her hand is a magic wand. She could be dreaming him, for Hubbell is a cross between Rip Van Winkle and Sleeping Beauty, an apparitional man (not unlike the somnambulistic Travis in Wim Wenders' *Paris, Texas*) posing as real.[63] Besotted, Katie pulls him forward, out of the dream and into the present, which may or may not be another dream. To have him, she will need to send herself back in time, into a past where she has no future. Into a future that is stuck in the past. The only way for Katie to be with Hubbell is for her to lose herself—to give up her time for his time.

61. As Julie Dash's *Daughters in the Dust* (1991) tells us: "What's past is prologue."

62. Though made in 1973, during second-wave feminism, *The Way We Were* is set in the past, commencing in the late 1930s and concluding in the 1950s. As I have argued in my books and feminist film courses, while male melancholia is a post-war phenomenon due to a perceived loss of socio-economic status by white heterosexual men, feminism, along with other civil rights movements, is an attempt to achieve a previously non-existent status. By setting the film in a pre-feminist past, *The Way We Were* avoids the feminist present in which it was made. And yet, despite the film's prevailing legacy as a "great" love story, it is impossible to view Hubbell without the film's '70s lens, which exposes and dates both his weakness and mediocrity—along with Katie's strength and tenac-

ity—by putting it into sociohistorical context.

63. Hubbell's ability to sleep through anything, including sex, is indicative of his unshakeable melancholia, general apathy, and resignation. Given *The Way We Were*'s dramatic structure, it is possible that he may even have slept through his entire 20-year relationship with Katie, or that their relationship is simply Katie's fantasy—a dream. Though writing specifically about post-millennial masculinity, in *Ghost Faces*, film theorist David Greven argues that historical masculinity is simultaneously "rooted in time and timeless." He terms this Gothic masculinity and neo-Irving masculinity, referring to Washington Irving's "Rip Van Winkle," in which a Dutch-American villager falls asleep in the Catskills mountains of colonial America and wakes up 20 years later, having missed the American Revolution. *The Way We Were*, a period film, also evades the feminist revolution by withdrawing into the past.

The Way We Were's misguided romantic allegory is an unwitting metaphor for the time-warp that is sexism. In the closing time-lapse, a match-dissolve bleeds into a static shot of Katie's mournful face after her marriage to Hubbell ends for good. A montage of changing seasons represents her grief.[64] Months—or years?—pass across her face in the same way that months or years flash across Hubbell's at the start of the film. As Katie's younger self fades from the screen, she is teleported to a future in which she unexpectedly re-encounters Hubbell again on the streets of New York City. Her life with Hubbell time-jumps into a life without Hubbell. Time has braced her for this. She is longer waiting (Godard: "I am no longer waiting for the train."). Katie's time with Hubbell has been in vain, a fate that befalls a certain kind of passionate, uncompromising woman whose persistence and tenacity when it comes to love and desire always works against her—what Jeanne Moreau, playing one of the three Fates of Cinema, refers to as "Ms.-en-scène" in Agnes Varda's *One Hundred and One Nights*. It is the same crisis of fate that will repeat itself fourteen years later in *Broadcast News*, with the more up-to-date, hurried Jane. Like Jane and Tom, Katie and Hubbell's irresolvable differences endure *across* time. *The Way We Were* ends the way it begins. The past is the future.

64. In *Dialogues*, Gilles Deleuze tells Claire Parnet that desire is always running through time: "Do you realize how simple a desire is? Sleeping is a desire. Walking is a desire. Listening to music, or making music, or writing, are desires. A spring, a winter, are desires."

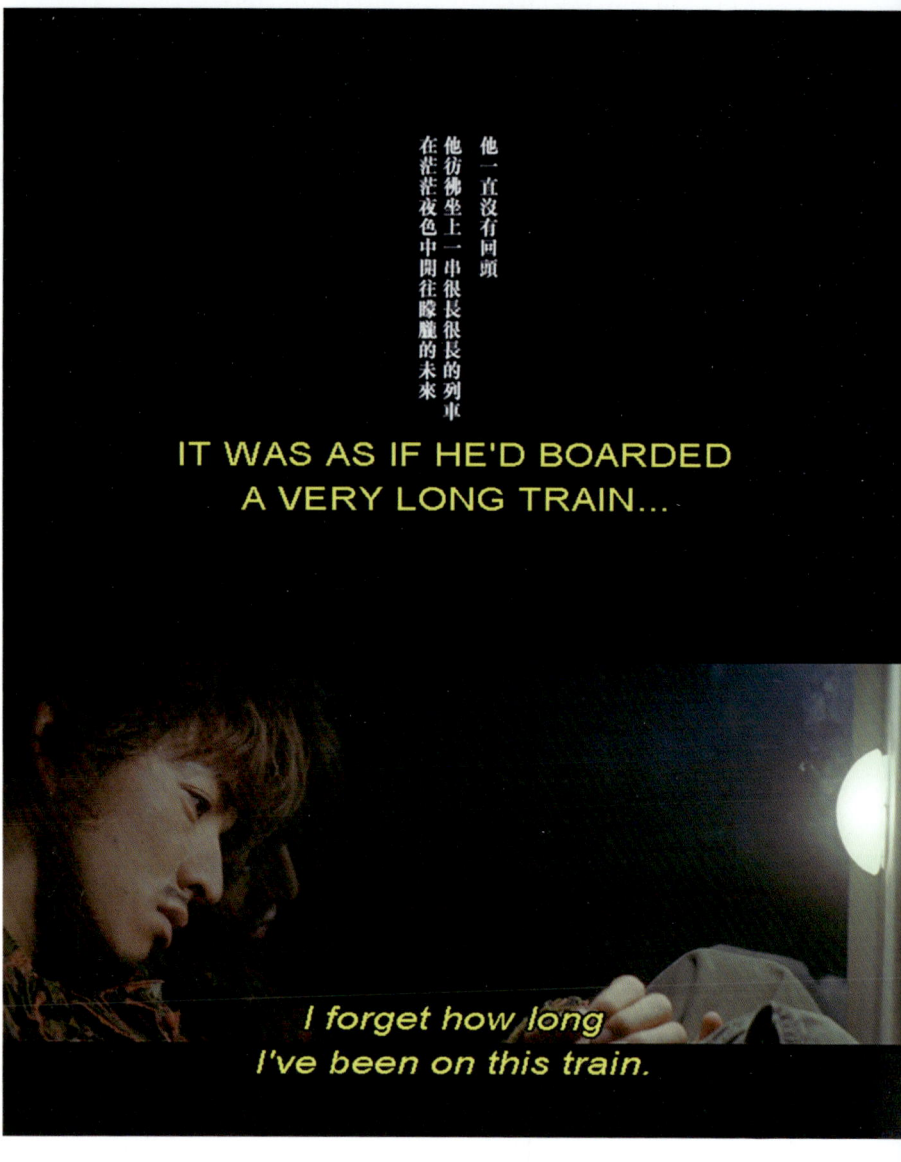

他一直沒有回頭
他彷彿坐上一串很長很長的列車
在茫茫夜色中閛往瞭朧的未來

IT WAS AS IF HE'D BOARDED
A VERY LONG TRAIN...

I forget how long
I've been on this train.

In Wong Kar-wai's romantic sci-fi *2046*, the future is the past and the hi-tech mystery train that teleports the characters in Wong's futuristic city of memories is once again, as Godard tells us, both the origin of cinema and the future of cinema. In Wong's cinematic future, everyone is stranded in an emotional past they can neither return to nor forget. Every time-jump forward brings them back to a lost love. "Why would there be the year 2046 and the city of 2046?" Wong asks? *2046* is built on the time-jump from *In the Mood for Love* (the original Chinese title means "Flowery Years"), in which, Wong explains, the enamored Chow "was still in 1963. But in 2046, it was already 1966, three years later … *2046* is about how person faces his future with all the things that happened in his past."

In *2046*, the hi-tech future is a sentimental city of memory. But 2046 is also a hotel room, right next to 2047, the one Chow rents. 2046 "is the room [Chow] longs to live in because a long time ago he had a love story that happened in room 2046, at another place. The room, like the city, represents the love memories he had in the past," explains Wong. The future is what happened before as well as what will happen again. The future is a high-speed train that arrives at the past faster and faster. "All the cyber elements in the movie are actually [Chow's] own imagination. An imagination of a man from 1966." Chow is a martial arts novelist turned science-fiction writer—what Wong calls a "future writer." As the genre of failed mourning, science-fiction is "actually the pieces of [Chow's] everyday life," reconstructed and rearranged. Wong reveals that he originally planned to make *2046* before 1997, when Hong Kong's "50 years unchanged regime" was often talked about. "50 years from 1997 would be 2046. I think it's interesting to use this number as the theme of our movie."

PART IV:
TIME STAMPS

"You're marking time."
— *Thief*

Despite the endless time stamps in David Fincher's *Zodiac*, the 2007 epic crime narrative is also denied a time cure. A presentist film[65] disguised as a period film, every passing hour that is obsessively and retroactively logged on-screen weighs on both the characters and audience alike. The suspense at the center of *Zodiac*'s narrative sprawl is that time solves nothing. In every scene, Fincher compulsively stamps a new anticlimactic date and hour onto the screen. Yet the identity of the Zodiac Killer is never confirmed. Instead we get suspicion, paranoia, obsession, red tape. A national mood, endless cataloging, lives ruined and derailed. Decades go by. Case files swell. Theories accumulate. Marriages end. Heartbreak is the systemic failure and disillusionment that comes with the unrelenting feedback loop of modern progress. Time is ticking, but time never stops ticking. Time is without time. In the nearly three-hour thriller, detectives patrol crime scenes—still on the Zodiac case years later, still waiting to solve the Zodiac murders. This is the movie's enormous contribution to the crime genre: an unremitting counting without countdown.

A far cry from the procedurally succinct *Dirty*

65. *Zodiac* was shot with Thomson Viper FilmStream high-definition (HD) video cameras, making it one of the first Hollywood features shot with the uncompressed-HD-to-drive digital-acquisition system. "[The concern] was mostly about workflow and how we were going to ingest the data," says Fincher. "It was also about getting used to watching things through a 32-inch LCD HD monitor and being able to direct from that. The image is kind of flat and green, but it offers an immediacy that allows you to hone and shape the image. And it's all in real time, so when you've shot the shot, you know you have it."

Harry and *Death Wish* movies made in the 1970s and 1980s, *Zodiac*'s drawn-out post-millennial fatigue offers no catharsis or solution—no hero or criminal.[66] *Zodiac* is exemplary of the ruthless presentism of post-narrative life.

Jonathan Crary:

> [24/7] is a time that no longer passes … Behind the vacuity of the catchphrase, 24/7 is a static redundancy that disavows its relation to the rhythmic and periodic textures of human life. It connotes an arbitrary, uninflected schema of a week, extracted from any unfolding of variegated or cumulative experience. To say "24/365," for example, is simply not the same, for this introduces an unwieldy suggestion of an extended temporality in which something might actually *change*, in which unforeseen events might happen [my emphasis].

When *Zodiac*'s Transamerica Pyramid montage occurs, a 30-second sped-up time-lapse of the construction of San Francisco's famous landmark, scored by Marvin Gaye's "Inner City Blues" (1971),[67] nothing comes of it. 11 months have passed. After the montage, the caption "One year later" appears at the bottom of the screen, stamped across the arms of a crestfallen Paul Avery (Robert Downey Jr.), a reporter for the *San Francisco Chronicle*. The rapid time-keeping sequence illustrates the City's transition into a presentist era via the digital construction of a

66. In 1972, there were still 2,300 suspects. That same year, Fincher has the Zodiac detectives sit through a fictional version of the case in the form of a special police screening of *Dirty Harry*, in which the crimes are solved and the killer is caught by one vigilante cop, Harry Callahan, inspector David Toschi's cinematic alter ego. Toschi, who storms out of the screening, is "frustrated at seeing his daily grind sensationalized on-screen," writes Adam Nayman in "Unsolved Mystery." Daily grind is a perfect way to describe what the digital-era Zodiac is usurping in its reference to analog-era police procedurals, like *Dirty Harry*. Grayson tells Toschi, "The killer gets shot in the chest. That's how [the movie] ends." And another inspector joshes Toschi, "Dave! That Harry Callahan did a hell of a job with your case." "Yeah. No need for due process, right?" Toschi fires back. When Grayson tries to

149

corporate landmark.⁶⁸ As a post-millennial film, the CGI time-jump represents the horrific scale of a new financial order as well as the cultural acceleration of time. This new class order emerges at the same time as the Zodiac murders.⁶⁹ It is when: "Old San Francisco, early '60s San Francisco, changes into '70s San Francisco," states Fincher, who spent his childhood in the Bay Area. The Transamerica Pyramid, which took three years to build in real life (1969 – 1972), takes 30 seconds to assemble in Fincher's movie.⁷⁰ Extended time becomes a blip. San Francisco goes from being a "city of mystery," as one TV journalist reporting on the Zodiac murders put it in 1969, to being the future city of the dot-com era, unleashing the Godzilla of 24/7 capitalism onto the once-countercultural city.

console Toschi by telling him, "You're gonna catch him," Toschi answers, "Pal, they're already making movies about it." After the screening, four more years go by. These four years, recorded as a black-screen time-jump, are not accounted for. While *Dirty Harry* runs for 1 hour and 43 minutes Zodiac's run-time is 2 hours and 42 minutes. The four-year time-jump also takes the form of an audio montage of different songs, "finally taking the movie from mono to stereo," Fincher explains. In this case, time moves forward in the form of sound. Fincher refers to the end of his movie as "the end of the '70s." In an interview about his memoir, *My Dark Places*, crime writer James Ellroy explains that in the "standard crime fiction sensibility," the vigilante is "usually a noble loner working against authority." Another term for this is "hero cop."

67. "Bad breaks, setbacks" is one of the lyrics in Gaye's song and can be heard during the time-lapse sequence. Scoring the time-lapse with Gaye's song adds a political dimension to the fast-forward, as does the architecture itself. Time enters the diegetic narrative via the nondiegetic. Fincher could have chosen any building to construct, but he chose the Transamerica Pyramid skyscraper. The building represents a financial absolutism that alters the future of temporality itself; the corporate remaking of a once-counterculture city—what Martin Scorsese calls the "mystery of old San Francisco." In *Zodiac*, San Francisco is a landscape of present shock that Fincher absorbed from his own childhood, but also from Hitchcock's eroticization of San Francisco in his film *Vertigo*. What is left behind is not simply the unsolved Zodiac case, but an entire era. In its reimagining of *Vertigo*, *Basic Instinct* (1992)—also set in San Francisco—detective Nick Curran makes a phone call from a payphone while the Transamerica Pyramid—now complete—looms in the background, reminding us of the Zodiac cold case. Nick himself lives directly across from the tower.

68. In his video essay, on Fincher's *Zodiac*: "The Masterpiece (the Directors Series)" for Indie Film Hustle TV, Cameron Beyl notes that Fincher also portrays a city in transition by "showing cranes in the skyline, holes in the ground waiting to be filled" before we even see the famous construction montage of the Transamerica Pyramid tower.

69. The grossly named Salesforce Tower, measuring at 1,070 feet, has been the tallest building in San Francisco as of 2018.

70. All the blood in the movie was also digitally manufactured making blood a synthetic computer-generated special effect.

151

While in *Dirty Harry* (1971), time—romanticized as a loss of traditional values—is ideologically recouped and condensed into a single vigilante hero, *Zodiac* (2007) uses the numbing dispensation of an extended temporality (the three-decade timespan of the unsolved Zodiac case) and the bureaucratic management of time (conflicting jurisdictional regulations. Or as James Ellroy refers to it, "jurisdictional fuck-up"[71]) to track duration and overload. "I was concerned about the amount of non-cinematic information that had to be conveyed on-screen," Harris Savides, Fincher's cinematographer, explains. By non-cinematic, Savides means time. "I told David [Fincher] we had to figure out ways to make these scenes interesting and cinematic, but our solution was the opposite." Fincher refers to this non-cinematic information as "the mundane." "The opposite," in this case, is all the non-cinematic information that *Dirty Harry* cuts out and *Zodiac*

71. *Zodiac* producer, Brad Fischer, says "a multi-jurisdictional homicide investigation was, like, unheard of … It took them 13 months to get a search warrant for Arthur Leigh Allen's trailer. This is 13 months after actually interrogating him in his place of work."

leaves in, as evidenced by the special police screening of *Dirty Harry* that takes place in the middle of *Zodiac*.

In the scene, Fincher places his main characters in the theater of the meta-film, forcing them into the audience role. In one world, the Zodiac case gets solved in 1 hour and 43 minutes. In the other, which runs 2 hours and 42 minutes, it doesn't get solved. In the screening scene, *Dirty Harry*'s and *Zodiac*'s running times overlap, each sharing each other's time, in the way that analog and digital time also coexist in Fincher's film. Only a minute before, Captain Martin Lee, David Toschi's boss, had proposed an intermission for Toschi, "What do you want? Time off? ... Take some time off ... See a movie." The movie we—and Toschi—see (mostly hear) for roughly 22 seconds, is *Dirty Harry*. And the time at which we see it is at 1 hour and 37 minutes into *Zodiac*, six minutes shorter than *Dirty Harry*'s running time. Like with Fincher's time-crossed lovers in *The Curious Case of Benjamin Button* (2008), in *Zodiac*, for six minutes, analog (*Dirty Harry*) and digital (*Zodiac*) "meet somewhere in the middle."

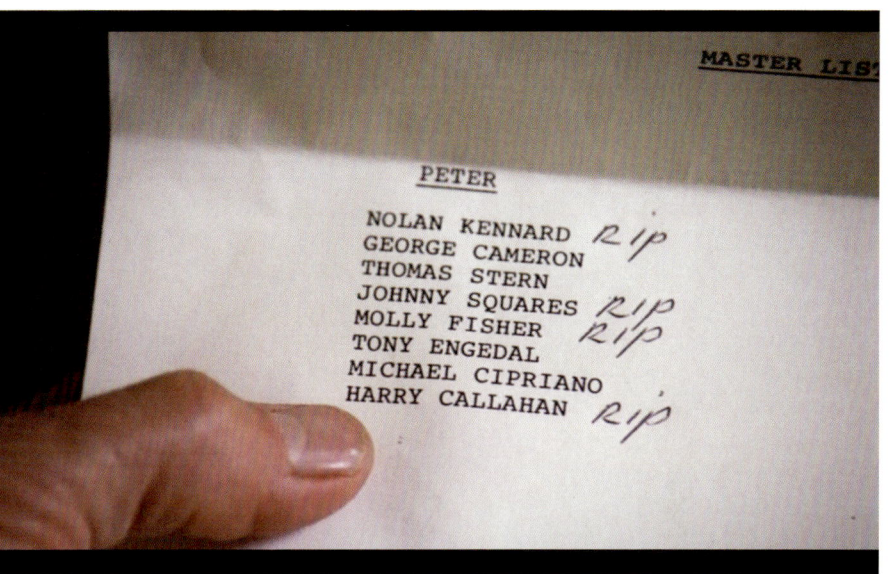

In *Dirty Harry*, the rogue Harry Callahan swallows time, creating his own speed and his own rules. In *Zodiac*, inspector David Toschi storms out of the *Dirty Harry* screening while continuing to adhere to Fincher's non-cinematic police protocol and masculinity. In a later scene, Toschi tells *San Francisco Chronicle* cartoonist, Robert Graysmith, "Easy, Dirty Harry," when Graysmith begins to emotionally unravel, deviating from procedural protocol in his vigilante pursuit of the Zodiac Killer. Although both *Dirty Harry* and *Zodiac* happen in the cinematic imaginary, Fincher differentiates the two approaches via his relentless, often anesthetizing formalization of time.[72] A human time-lapse, Harry Callahan, along with Paul Kersey, the once mild-mannered New York liberal architect turned vigilante in *Death Wish* (1974), beats time to save the day (days which were stolen from Kersey when his wife was raped and murdered).

In *Zodiac*, no matter how much time passes, the Zodiac case remains unsolved. It forces its melancholic male characters into a state of unending impotence and delay. The digitization of the passage of time that enters moviemaking and usurps the cinematic, becomes the film's great unspoken wound; a conclusion and formal approach that only makes sense because time itself is being mourned and phased-out. In the film's commentary, screenwriter James Vanderbilt jokingly refers to *Zodiac*'s deluge of time stamps as, "These fucking chyrons, *man*. We had to go through these so … *many* … times. I mean, like up to *release* … we were just rewriting and rewriting and rewriting."[73] The Chyron manufacturing company's original spelling of chyron

72. In *Zodiac Deciphered*, Zodiac screenwriter, James Vanderbilt, states: "One of things that was really important to us was when people would see this movie and go, 'Why didn't they catch him? Why didn't they get him?' We really wanted to show how hard it is to get a search warrant… That's something that doesn't really get explored. What is the drudge work that these guys have to go through?… The more you're able to show that, the more heroic." This "drudge" logic completely negates the logic of the vigilante, who takes both the law and time into his own hands, bypassing procedure. As Harry Callahan puts it in the 1973 sequel, *Magnum Force*, "Nothing wrong with shooting long as the right people get shot."

73. Fincher resumes his obsessive time stamping in his new Old-Hollywood period film, *Mank* (2020).

was Chiron. In Greek mythology, Chiron, a centaur, was the son of the Titan Cronus and the sea nymph Oceanid Philyra (Apollo was Chiron's foster father). Chiron's bloodline gifted him with supernatural powers of healing. In the myth of Chiron, the centaur receives a wound in his thigh. The wound is so painful that Chiron wants to die. But since he is immortal, he cannot end his life. In exchange for his immortality, Chiron is spared his pain and is given permission to die. In astrology, along with Juno, Ceres, Pallas, and Vesta, Chiron is one of the major asteroids and is referred to as the "wounded healer." In each person's natal chart, a zodiac sign and house placement for Chiron tells us not only where a wound is located, but what form and remedy it might take over the course of one's life. Through his use of time graphics—chyrons—Fincher inadvertently conjures the myth of Chiron, simultaneously addressing and inflicting the wounds of time on his viewers over and over again. Serial killers also excel at repetitive wounding. In astrology, a minimum of three planets in a sign or house are required in order to form a stellium. In modern criminology, explains Fincher, "You don't have a serial killer until you have three murders."

Observing *Zodiac*'s Lake Berryessa greeting card nearly 40 years later in the documentary *This Is the Zodiac Speaking*, criminal profiler Sharon Pagaling Hagan, remarks, "[The Zodiac] was into time. He's continually telling us how far something is; how long it's been." The Berryessa timecard states the following:

> Vallejo
> 12-20-68
> 7-4-69
> September 27-69-6:30
> by knife

For serial killers, patterns and numbers are significant. In his retelling of the case, Fincher takes the Zodiac's approach, offering an excess of time stamps (time-telling devices that act in tandem with Zodiac's cyphers to the *SF Chronicle*) that indicate both a fixation with and anxiety over present shock. What is significant about Zodiac's Lake Berryessa timecard is the way in which it both establishes and breaks a pattern of notation. In the timecard, written on a car door, Zodiac presents three different systems of time-telling. In the first two instances, only the date is listed. In the third, he spells out the month of September and adds the time of day. Place—Vallejo—is a locational umbrella for all three dates/murders; as is knife, which, like place, bookends the dates, but seems to apply only to the last murder, as the others were executed with a gun. Fincher echoes Zodiac's irregular timecards throughout the film, establishing patterns and breaking patterns, adding new details and withholding old details, something Toschi will come to observe later about Zodiac's killing patterns.[74]

The whole world is a homicide victim, Father.

In an episode of his podcast series, *Ways of Hearing*, musician Damon Krukowski reflects on musical time: "What musicians' terms like rubato, swing, and groove acknowledge is that time is experienced, not counted like a clock … Machines have a different sense of time." By different, Krukowski means different from *humans*. The difference between the time in which *Zodiac* is made (the digital present) and the time with which *Zodiac* is preoccupied (the analog past) is arguably the film's de facto narrative. *Zodiac* not only opens on a time-themed song, Three Dog Night's "Easy to Be Hard," but with the hauntological crackle of vinyl that precedes the song, which was recorded in 1969, the year of Zodiac's first reported murder. The hiss of the 11-second intro to "Easy to Be Hard" is the only thing we can hear while the Warner Bros. Pictures logo flashes on-screen. It takes 23 seconds of running time for a panorama of a Vallejo skyline on the evening of July 4, 1969, to appear.[75]

74. In an email, the writer Stephen Beachy tells me that "criminality is a form, one of the major forms of masculinity."

75. Consequently, Fincher's second daytime (more high-speed) opening montage takes place in San Francisco "4 weeks later," as the time stamp tells us, and is, in my mind, an obvious homage to the opening of *The Maltese Falcon* (1941). My feeling is that much of Fincher's time constructions and slow pacing are inspired by Fred

Zinnemann's superb 1973 political thriller, *The Day of the Jackal*. While Fincher makes obsessive use of time stamps to build his crime narrative, Zinnemann uses a vast array of analog clocks. In both cases, the frequency of usage accelerates as the films progress. In his review, Roger Ebert wrote that *The Day of the Jackal* is "put together like a fine watch." Both films are about the art and duration of procedure. Though I have searched online for a mention of *Jackal*'s influence on Fincher and found nothing, in my mind, the comparison is undeniable.

In *Zodiac*, all the time notations result in a cutting pattern. Fincher counts *too* much. Dates and places are excessively noted. There are time-jumps, time stamps, time-lapses, musical montages, cyphers, watches, and clocks. All pile up on themselves producing a "static redundancy" (Crary). The late twentieth century serial killer is a hieroglyphic system that requires decoding. In the movie, time is at stake, but time is also cancelling time. Instead of showing us what happens, who is behind it, or how to correct it, Fincher, like the Zodiac Killer, only shows us "how long it's been."[76] Time is incessantly counted and displayed, but the situation remains fixed. As a throwback format, the time stamp is the most analog aspect of Fincher's protracted movie. And yet, the sped-up and redundant nature of his usage, as well as the excessive frequency, belongs to the digital network, where time is absent via its constant presence.

76. In the *Zodiac* commentary, Robert Downey Jr., who plays *SF Chronicle* reporter, Paul Avery, tells Jake Gyllenhaal, "The movie is about taking its time." In 1991, discussing his trying portrayal of Jim Morrison in Oliver Stone's *The Doors*, Val Kilmer stated that movies are about endurance, which suggests duration.

In the first 30 minutes of Zodiac, a total of ten time stamps and time-jumps appear:

1. July 4, 1969, Vallejo, CA.
2. 4 weeks later, San Francisco, CA.
3. 12 hours later, Sonoma, CA, Skaggs Island Naval Intelligence Center
4. 6 hours later, San Francisco, CA, Federal Bureau of Investigation.
5. 5 hours later, Langley, VA, Central Investigation Agency.
6. 12 hours later, Salinas, CA, Breakfast nook of Donald and Bettye Harden.
7. 3 days later, San Francisco, CA. (Graysmith tells Avery, "I've been here nine months.")
8. 1½ months later, Napa, CA, September 27, 1969. (Time stamp is reinstated in Zodiac's Berryessa crime scene timecard.)
9. 2 weeks later, San Francisco, CA, October 11, 1969.
10. At the Paul Stine crime scene on Washington and Cherry, Toschi looks at his watch on two occasions. He wishes Inspector Armstrong, his partner, a happy birthday.

From 31–60 minutes, the time stamps and time-jumps accelerate in frequency to every scene:

11. 3 days later, San Francisco, CA.
12. 10 hours later, Sacramento, CA, Bureau of Criminal Identification and Investigation.
13. 12 hours later, San Francisco, CA.
14. 2 days later, San Francisco, CA.
15. Wall clock in lobby behind Inspector Armstrong and Inspector Toschi as they discuss the Zodiac case.
16. 2 days later, San Francisco, CA, October 22, 1969.
17. Clocks at *The Jim Dunbar Show* TV station; calendar of the year 1969 behind Paul Avery at the *San Francisco Chronicle*; shot of wristwatch worn by a San Francisco reporter watching *The Jim Dunbar Show*; wall clock.

18. 2½ weeks later, San Francisco, CA (The same row of international wall clocks at *San Francisco Chronicle* appear).
19. 1½ months later, San Francisco, CA.
20. 2½ months later, Highway 132 near Modesto, CA, March 22, 1970.

60–90 minutes, additional references to time begin to appear:

21. One-minute music montage of Zodiac press and publicity. Begins on March 23, 1970, Modesto CA. Local newspapers with dates and locations are featured. Montage contains voice-over narration by three different characters (Toschi, Armstrong, and *Chronicle* crime reporter, Paul Avery) and also features the following time stamps: 30 days later, San Francisco, CA; 8 days later, San Francisco, CA; 2 months later, San Francisco, CA; the dates and times Zodiac has listed in his letters to the *Chronicle* are read as non-diegetic narrtion and superimposed onto walls as floating cryptograms (it is a Zodiac world at this point); wall of international clocks at the *Chronicle*.
22. 4 weeks later, San Francisco, CA. Graysmith's watch; at Morti's Bar, Graysmith tells Avery there have been "4 letters in 3 months."

reme C
cused of m
ed because of
rror. Page 2.

e fied
mmission
spaper
lly" and
e loss
Regen

n Fran

★   SATU

New Cop

23. At the *San Francisco Chronicle* archive, Avery shows Graysmith a date—Saturday, June 20, 1970—listed in a back issue of the *Chronicle* to prove that the Zodiac has taken credit for crimes he did not commit, introducing a new component to the case: the Zodiac's interest in publicity. The camera shoots the newspaper in closeup, with Avery's finger pointing to the date.
24. Armstrong and Toschi on a night stakeout in the police car. Armstrong announces that the Zodiac hasn't made a "peep in four months," echoing Graysmith at Morti's two scenes prior. Then Toschi wishes Bill a happy birthday again, indicating that it has been a year since the Stine murder on Washington and Cherry, when it was also Armstrong's birthday. The scene concludes with their car pulling away from what appears to be Washington and Cherry, and a closing time stamp: October 11, 1970, San Francisco, CA, the corner of Washington and Cherry, visually confirming the already-established location.
25. 2½ weeks later, San Francisco, CA.
26. Graysmith's first blind date with Melanie, his future wife. Graysmith, who is normally very punctual, arrives at the restaurant and exclaims, "How late am I?" (more a declaration than a question) when he sits down, soaked from the rain. "Just a few minutes, really," Melanie politely assures.[77] Time is not specified (i.e., we do not how late Graysmith actually is).
27. Melanie and Graysmith stay up all night waiting for Avery to call after he has driven to another city to meet with an anonymous

77. The shock of this date scene is when Graysmith tells Melanie that Paul Avery is married, which until this moment, would never have occurred to me given the way Avery is portrayed in the film. All his time is dedicated to his job and to drinking all night. This in itself is telling: men who have no relation to anything other than their work, other men, and addiction, can nevertheless find women to marry. In her memoir, *I'm Over All That: And Other Confessions*, Shirley MacLaine wrote the following observation about working with her male co-stars in film: "They avoided their own search by becoming other men on the screen."

Zodiac tipster. The scene is introduced with the singsong of a clock striking some unspecified crepuscular hour.
28. There is a small clock beside the TV set that reports new information on the Zodiac case, "regarding the only homicide in Riverside County's history, a 1966 Southern California murder that Avery now believes was the Zodiac's first victim."
29. November 18, 1970.
30. 2 hours later, Riverside, CA (Riverside precinct shares that "Cheri Jo Bates attended Riverside Community College. She studies at the library on the night of October 30th, 1966. She leaves with an unidentified male at closing, 9:00 p.m. ... A typewritten confession was sent to the Riverside Press Enterprise on November 29th, a month after Bates' murder." Date of confession letter—November 29, 1966—is then shown on camera and read out loud). Outside, in the parking lot, Avery taunts Toschi by evoking time: "Hey, Bullitt! Been a year and a half, you gonna catch this fucking guy or not?"
31. 45-second music voice-over montage of false Zodiac leads and fake confessions given to detectives Toschi and Armstrong. One source tells Toschi, "You're a cop, do the math."
32. Inspector Armstrong takes notes during an interview with informant Don Cheney. Armstrong's hand is seen writing a date on a yellow legal pad: July 26, 1971. Then, once the interview commences a couple of seconds later, a time stamp appears on-screen: "8 months later, Torrance, CA, July 26, 1971," recapping the date we already saw scribbled on the notebook. Cheney tells Armstrong that he "put the story together about a year ago," when he recognized his co-worker, Arthur Leigh Allen. In another room, a wall clock is visible during the interview. Armstrong asks Cheney to confirm that the conversation he had about Zodiac "took place on January 1st, 1968."
33. Armstrong and Toschi discuss Cheney's testimony. Armstrong mentions that Cheney first talked to the police about Arthur Leigh Allen on January 30, 1970.
34. 1 day later, Rodeo, CA, August 4, 1971. Armstrong, Toschi, and Sgt. Jack Mulanax, inform Arthur Leigh Allen that an informant

notified them that Allen made "certain statements 11 months prior to the first Zodiac murder." The three interrogating officers ask Allen if he was ever in "Southern California at any time in 1966?" A wall clock shows the time is 9:37 am. A close-up of Allen's Zodiac watch (a brand) is shot from Toschi's POV. Allen fondles his watch. Toschi askes Allen if he can see his watch. Allen takes his watch off and gives it to Toschi. Allen says, "It was a Christmas gift from my mother two years ago." Allen's watch gets passed around the table. Each officer examines the watch. We see different hands (all donning wrist watches) holding Allen's watch. Toschi hands Allen's watch back to him and thanks him for his "time."

35. 10 hours later, Vallejo, CA.
36. 30-second visual time-lapse of Transamerica Pyramid construction. The highspeed compilation indicates that we are now in the technological future.
37. 1 year later, San Francisco, CA. Avery asks Graysmith to get a drink with him. Graysmith reminds Avery that it is "Ten in the morning."

Four years later

90–120 minutes:

38. September 7, 1972, Vallejo, CA. Allen's sister-in-law tells Armstrong that she had seen Allen for the first time in 9 months. Toschi and Armstrong ask Captain Martin Lee to search Allen's trailer in Santa Rosa; Lee chides that it's been 11 months since they interrogated Allen.
39. September 14, 1972, Santa Rosa, CA, Sunset Trailer Park, Space A-7.
40. Captain Martin Lee asks a distraught Toschi, "Hey, what do you want? Time off?"
41. In the Director's Cut, the time-jump consists of the following transition: a nearly 2-minute blackout audio montage of news broadcast and dialogue is presented in voice over to summarize all the time that has passed: End of the Vietnam War, Charles Manson murders, Chowchilla kidnapping, death of Chairman Mao, Watergate, kidnapping of Patricia Hearst, Jimmy Hoffa, Son of Sam. The screen remains dark during this time. History is reduced to a series of crimes and deaths. Then, in the middle of the voice-overs, the time-jump, "4 years later" appears at the bottom of the screen. There is a song change for every historic announcement. Fincher spins and samples history like a DJ. This 2-minute pause is Fincher's version of an intermission. (Note: This sequence has no visuals and only appears in the Director's Cut, which is 4 minutes longer than the theatrical release. The montage is restored on the DVD, but was trimmed from the released film because the studio felt the film was already too long and inaccessible.) Critic Scott Tobias calls this sequence "the dead years ... It is the film's documentation of these fallow years that sets it apart from other procedurals of its kind." In the theatrical cut, Graysmith meets Toschi for the first time at the *Dirty Harry* screening. He tells Toschi,"You're gonna catch him." After this scene, there is a 7-second blackout (intermission) before the time-jump "4 years later" appears onscreen.
42. When Graysmith pays Avery a visit at his home, the time-jump, "4 years later," is echoed by Avery telling Graysmith, "It was 4 years ago. Let it fucking go."

43. October 11, 1977, San Francisco, CA, the corner of Washington and Cherry (based on the way Toschi and Armstrong have been shown sitting in their cars on Washington and Cherry before, we are now painfully aware of where we are and why it is significant. Yet Fincher still notes the location).

44. One-minute montage of Graysmith at the Vallejo Police Department pouring over thousands of Zodiac files. Close up of Graysmith massaging his sore neck with his left hand to indicate he has been doing this for hours. His watch is also emphasized in the shot in order to suggest the many hours this is taking as well as the amount of files that have been amassed on the Zodiac case. A wall clock is the first thing we see in the right-hand corner of the frame when Graysmith shoots out of the precinct. We see the clock but we cannot see the time.

45. Graysmith visits the home of Marvin Belli to ask him some questions about the Zodiac. He is kept waiting for a long time. When Belli's maid apologies for Belli's tardiness, Graysmith looks at his watch and tells her that he has "only been waiting two hours." Graysmith and Belli's maid go on to discuss the dates and years of the Zodiac's phone call to Belli's home, which apparently occurred on the Zodiac's birthday, December 18.
46. Graysmith comes home. He finds his wife Melanie working. He asks her how her day was and she simply replies, "Long." They also discuss the time Graysmith plans to take off work ("1 hour") to go to Sacramento, which Melanie tells him is actually 2 hours away from San Francisco.

120–162 minutes:

47. April 25, 1978, San Francisco, CA.
48. Graysmith's two sons ("colleagues") begin to help their father with the Zodiac "timeline," asking, "What about September 26, 1970?" They list a number of other potentially significant dates.
49. August 9, 1979, San Francisco, CA. Avery, now ill with pulmonary emphysema, watches the evening news at Morti's, which announces the span of time that has passed since the *Chronicle* received the last Zodiac letter: 10 years. Despite what Avery tells Graysmith about the job of the reporter being to report only on the "day," otherwise it is "old news," the etymology of the word chronicle itself is rooted in chronology—*khronos*—which is to say, a longer cumulation of time ("Historical account of facts or events in the order of time," (c. 1300), "To record in a chronicle, make a simple record of occurrences in their order of time." (c. 1400)).
50. Graysmith meets with Bob Vaughn, who appears to be running late since the scene opens with Graysmith looking at his watch as he stands outside in the pouring rain. When Graysmith gets spooked by Vaughn while visiting his home, he tells him, "I won't take any more of your time."
51. Graysmith comes home after his meeting with Vaughn to find his family has moved out. He goes into his children's bedroom, now

empty. In it, a child's drawing of a clock hangs on the wall. Graysmith turns to look at it for a split second before exiting the room.

52. Graysmith visits Linda del Buono (a friend of one of the Zodiac's victims) in San Joaquin prison. The guard tells Graysmith, "You've got five minutes," echoing *Drive*'s 5-minute window structure. In the next scene, Graysmith shows up at the Vallejo Police Department, begging to see a file. Sgt. Mulanx also tells Graysmith, "You got five minutes." This is Fincher's way of telling his audience, "We are running out of time." Sgt Mulanx echoes this fact by telling a now frantic Graysmith, "Our investigation into the subject is over."

53. Melanie comes home to hand Graysmith divorce papers as well as a photocopy of Arthur Leigh Allen's driver's license. Melanie and Graysmith discuss the night they met. Melanie calls their marriage "the date that didn't end."

54. Graysmith and Toschi meet at a diner one last time to retrace the Zodiac case. The go over all the significant details and dates again. Toschi tells Graysmith that what is true cannot be proven.

55. December 20, 1983, Vallejo, CA. Graysmith visits ACE hardware store where Allen now works. Oddly, the wall calendar that Allen is standing in front of when Graysmith walks in to silently confront him, is dated February 1980, not December 1983. Time is lagging three years behind. The Zodiac Killer is now running years ahead.

56. 7½ years later, August 16, 1991, Ontario, CA. Graysmith's book on the Zodiac is now a bestseller. Vallejo detective meets with Michael Mageau, the Zodiac's first surviving victim, to see if Mageau can identify the man who shot him. Mageau tells Vallejo PD, George Bawart, who's taken over for Jack Mulanax, "It's been 22 years. I don't know how I can help you." The passage of time is then emphasized again when Mageau says: "The last time I saw [Arthur Leigh Allen's] face, it was July 4, 1969." The movie comes full circle by ending on the film's first time-stamp as well as Donovan's "Hurdy Gurdy Man."

Fincher's never-ending title cards and repetitive references to time are tautologies of the Zodiac's crime puzzles. By overchronicling and overcataloguing every instance of the film's plot, even when the very progression of the diegetic narrative (the sequence of scenes) makes the progression of time redundant, Fincher's monotonous surfeit of temporal orientation tells us that time is not the answer. More precisely, cinema is not the solution to the wounding of time; a presentist, post-cinematic verdict that is symbolized by the repetitively wounding figure of the serial killer. Why, then, does Fincher want us to pay attention to such small—often obvious—increments of time *all the time*? In my compilation of the movie's 56 time-stamps, in which I attempted to recreate the obsessive iterations of Fincher's formal construction in order to study it, it becomes clear that for Fincher, scene changes—the move from interior shot to exterior shot; city to city; day to night; scene to scene; crime to crime—are simply not orienting *enough*.

TIME IS LUCK, WILL

"Scene after scene in *Zodiac* begins with a time code that places it not only in a historical context (month, day, year) but in relationship to the previous scene ('two days later,' 'three months later'), but these specifics don't lead to The Answer," writes Matt Zoller Seitz. "The movie's time stamp title cards ultimately prove as useless as the ones in *The Shining*."[78] The trope of the fated calendar—expressed as a fatal countdown—can be found in films as varied as F. W. Murnau's *Tabu*, *Psycho*, *Rosemary's Baby*, *The Shining*, *Day of the Dead*, *Memento*, and *Donnie Darko*. Film scholar Janet Bergstrom writes that "Fate speaks through the language of repetition." But what fate is Fincher trying to foresee in reverse? The criminalization of time? The birth and atomization of new death forms?

78. Hervé Guibert's line, "It's the sort of time that can't be measured in days" comes to mind here.

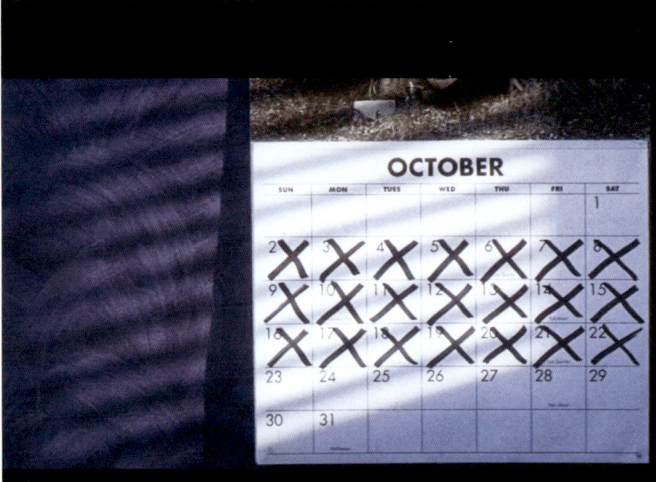

October 30 1988

(SIX HOURS REMAIN)

In *Zodiac*, time is forensic. The serial killer (who must kill more than three people in order to qualify) is also a time pattern. *Zodiac*'s countdown, as Seitz notes, is useless because nothing is leading us anywhere (both the case clues and the hours spent investigating them are dead ends); more importantly, much of the information has already been supplied by titles from previous scenes, or via the characters and visuals Fincher continues to count and recount in different ways. Take for example, Paul Avery at his *Chronicle* desk opening his mail. If it is the *San Francisco Chronicle*, why tell us we're in San Francisco over and over again? Why add California as well? If it is "2 days later," and if Inspector Toschi is sleeping at home when he receives a late-night phone call about the Zodiac, we already know we are in San Francisco because that is where we know Toschi lives; we can easily calculate the date based on the previous title stamp in the previous scene. If it is "2 days later," it is surely still 1969. If we do the math, that is, if we count all the other times Fincher has already clocked in prior scenes (scenes that may as well be clocks), as well as all the locations he has already established (if not through the chyrons, then visually through established locations), these excessive and overly precise time stamps are not only unnecessary, they are gratuitous. They also literally interrupt the viewer's immersion in the story; that is, in the diegetic flow (investigation/plot) by constantly reiterating what we already know, thereby forcing us, as *Zodiac*'s set decorator Victor Z. Zolfo points out, to focus on the passage of time rather than the plot. As Savides notes, to do so is also noncinematic; a way of delaying the story, which in this case will lead to the identity of a killer. Some of *Zodiac*'s more detailed time stamps also incorporate delay: the time stamps appear on screen in stages—time-released over a period of seconds—rather than all at once. However, if we take the film as a series of anti-elliptical calculations that, as Fincher explains in his 2017 discussion of his Netflix series *Mindhunter*, precede the FBI's invention of a criminal profiling system, then we see that the film's time stamps are the analog and jurisdictionally uncoordinated equivalent of a not-yet invented criminal computer database. *Mindhunter*, explains Fincher, "is on the tail of that frustration. We could say that the serial killer is perfect *timing* for the FBI."[79] (my emphasis). If the serial killer, and criminal history more generally, is a new form of time, as well as a new way of counting, then *Zodiac* confronts the epistemization and profiling of male violence as the beginning of the modern technological era by programming it as an electronic database.⁸⁰

Like *Zodiac*, Dziga Vertov's 1926 film, *A Sixth Part of the World*, features an ample number of titles. In "Man with a Movie Camera—Lines of Resistance,"⁸¹ Yuri Tsivian writes "[The 1920s] was the decade during which 'Do films need intertitles?' became an increasingly polarizing question, so no wonder Vertov got into crossfire. There were people who totally bought into this sort of poetical-political rhetoric, and there were those who found this style stilted or who, like Soviet formalist scholar Viktor Shklovsky, perceived in its titling technique a relapse into the era when a humdrum lecturer was needed to explain every image that flashed across the screen." In *A Sixth Part of the World*, Vertov's redundant titles replace optics, selectively telling us what we are seeing as we are seeing it. When a squirrel appears, the subtitle "Squirrel" also appears. But when the title "Caracul" appears, the camels in the frame are not cited, nor are the places in which these animals and objects reside. Other things are not named at all, or their pattern of titling varies—from generic to descriptive to poetic to narrative to instructive. As the film unfolds, the titles evolve into poetic absurdist riddles and commentary: "Fish;" "Your butter;" "Your tobacco;" "Where the bread ... like an incessant ribbon;" "And WHERE ... there isn't ANY road ... you can't meet anyone at all." Sometimes, like in *Zodiac*, the titles cease altogether. In *A Sixth Part of the World*, the repetition of the phrase, "I can see"—a global "sight" delivered by a worldly

79. In a 2018 podcast on Jeffrey Dahmer, the journalist Sarah Marshall describes the late-twentieth century serial killer—a now "dying industry"—as "the best PR for the FBI." Discussing Netflix's 2019 *Conversations with a Killer: The Ted Bundy Tapes*, Bill Simmons echoes Marshall on his podcast, calling the 1970s, "a gravy train for serial killers," and notes an additional reciprocity between the serial killer and law enforcement: "[Bundy] was a lawyer and working with police at one point, and had all this access to all these crimes. They basically gave him the blueprint for how to be the worst serial killer of the decade. So, he's reading all the information, and he's thinking, if I just do this and this and I move around to different states, nobody will ever catch me."

80. In the Amazon Prime docuseries, *Ted Bundy: Falling for a Killer* (2020),

camera eye—appears again and again. However, in Vertov's usage of the pronoun "You"—"You, in the grain to the knees;" "You, in the water to the knees;" "And YOU, the frozen sea on the Baltic Coasts"—he situates the viewer in the ideological and collectivist exposition of the titles. All things (titles) amount to industry. All industry amounts to "Us" and "All." The titles are a fragmentary aggregate of the larger narrative of industrial expansionism. The titles observe more than the camera by orienting it: "With MACHINES producing MACHINES." "For the EXPORT to countries of capital." "FAR AWAY."

Fincher's relapse into an excessive and varying titling technique eighty years later leaves us with the same question: "Do films need intertitles?" In both Vertov and Fincher's films, to name what is shown is not simply to be literal or redundant, it is to point to what is unclassifiable, ineffable, and insoluble via repetition. In *Zodiac*, intertitles are an investigative technique, a notational equivalent of the crime genre and leisure killing in the late twentieth century. As in Hitchcock's *Psycho*, where real-life crime is synonymous with cinematic genre, *Zodiac* captures the deadlock of genre itself. Fincher's achingly exact film demonstrates that genre can no longer provide a formal explanation for the innumerable ravages of post-narrative life under digital capitalism. The calendar becomes a cryptogram. *Zodiac* arrives at a critical juncture in time—the exact same moment that the cinematic becomes post-cinematic and Apple introduces the iPhone to the global market.[82] Both were released in 2007, within three months of each other. *Zodiac* gives us a telescopic view of the

Seattle journalist Knute Berger reflects on the relationship between late modernity and the evolution of vocational male crime: "When the interstates finally came to Seattle, it was a gamechanger. They allowed people to go farther, faster, and in a sense, more anonymously than in the past. It was giving you high-speed access to very rural and wilderness areas. The killer was using the highways in order to find victims." KNBC News producer Paul Skolnick confirms the boom of interstate criminal jet-setting in the docuseries *Night Stalker: The Hunt for a Serial Killer* (2021), which focuses on the mid-1980s Los Angeles serial killer Richard Ramirez: "He was 500 miles away and doing the same thing. This is a state wave of terror." Ramirez "spent his time studying maps of the City's freeways and neighborhoods, often driving around and sleeping in sto-

future-as-predatory algorithm by celebrating the existential crime-puzzle of its mysterious predecessor: the cipher.

len cars." Tellingly, the opening scene of David Fincher's *Zodiac* is filmed from the POV of a car window, making the car itself an extension of the predatory male gaze in late-twentieth century America. The car is a vehicle for voyeurism (we see this in Scorsese's *Taxi Driver*) and stalking, inextricable from the male predator's gaze. As Heidegger explains in his 1953 essay, "The Question Concerning Technology," technology and epistemology have always gone hand in hand: "From earliest times until Plato the word techne is linked with the word episteme. Both words are terms for knowing in the widest sense." Thus, just as the profiler needs technology (profiling databases) to know the killer, who himself is a product of postwar technological society, the postwar serial killer makes use of what technology has to offer in order to commit his crimes.

81. *Masterpieces of Modernist Cinema*, ed. Ted Perry. Indiana University Press, 2006

82. On January 9, 2007, at the Macworld Convention, Steve Jobs announced that the first iPhone would be released later that year, receiving substantial media attention. In the manifesto, "Activated Boredom," a creative consultancy with Kimberly Roberts, that "investigat[es] how younger generations are reappraising the physical world through a digitally native lens," Keaton Ventura states: "In 2020, The iPhone becomes a teenager. That means, to an arguable extent, that connectivity is finally coming of age. And in light of its maturation, the elder generations are freaking out. They thought unlimited access to more information would mean that every question would find an answer period. That things would make more sense, rather than less. There are, at least in perception, endless tradeoffs. With each new generation of iPhone, another deal is made with the Reaper. With every new software update, a childhood memory fades."

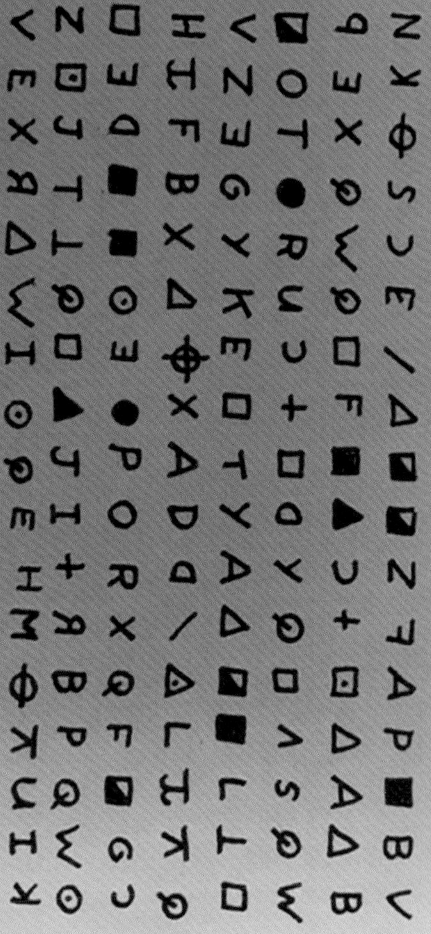

HER>pL^d YOB|cM+UZGW
()W--)S()+N⊞⊡K|
)⊡⊙K|GzMJY⏀●⊞①⊡
⊡N⊞⊙K●+1 zp⊞⊞⊡⊡JS*
AN+B PORXQF G)⊡
⊡⊙⊞+R/△ ⏀ ●⊞+LM
V⊞X⊡D W I ⊙P E H M ⏀ ⌐ I K

PART V:
RUBATO

"Time is like a clock in my heart."
—Culture Club, "Time (Clock of the Heart)"

The final act of *Zodiac* focuses on Robert Graysmith's solo investigation of the Zodiac. Time begins to slow down and speed up simultaneously. Fincher's notational pace slackens while the action accelerates. What, we should ask, is happening to time (and to Graysmith's life) during this part of the movie that makes Fincher decide to track it differently? What has happened to time—to the way it is passing in the final hour—that no longer makes it calculable in the same way? In *Zodiac*, writes Seitz, "Time changes everything but the narrative's forgone conclusion (or non-conclusion)." In *tempo rubato*, a type of tempo marking in music, the performer does not stick to the composer's strict rhythms. Unlike click tracks and drum machines, which "lock musical time to a clock," in *rubato*, time is flexible and unsteady. It happens (and changes) in real time. In *rubato*, adds Krukowski: "The performer is instructed to freely and expressively speed up or slow down at certain passages. In Italian, '*rubare*' means 'to steal' and '*tempo*' means 'time.' Therefore '*tempo rubato*' means the time of some measures are stolen by the others." Fincher does something similar with *Zodiac*. In the film, Fincher, like the Zodiac Killer, is inconsistent in his pattern of time codes. In the beginning of the film, time is both procedural, of the essence. On the clock. But when the case inadvertently falls to Graysmith at the end—when Graysmith *steals* the case—time suddenly turns vigilante. Off the clock. Like Harry Callahan in *Dirty Harry*, Graysmith is an element of inconsistency in the rest of the *Zodiac* narrative. He unofficially sneaks the investigation from its official and original investigators and becomes his own tempo marking.[83] The film's tempo now belongs to Graysmith. Graysmith is Toschi's "time off." Graysmith is *rubato*. This is confirmed by the time stamp—April 25, 1978, San Francisco, CA—that suddenly appears on-screen when Toschi is asked to call in on the police landline after a new Zodiac letter mentioning his name arrives at the *Chronicle*. The Zodiac, we are told, has been silent for 51 months and it has been a decade since the last cypher was sent. The investigation is "dead"; "Zodiac is long gone." Apart from David Shire's musical interludes that accelerate the pace during key moments of Graysmith's obsessive hunt, like the Zodiac Killer himself, the time stamps and locations largely disappear again until the very end of the film, when Graysmith visits the ACE hardware store where Arthur Leigh Allen, the main Zodiac suspect, is employed in 1983. "If you're watching for it, you feel the passage of time," states Zolfo. "And hopefully, if you're not watching for it, you feel the passage of time." Zolfo is right. Time works both ways in *Zodiac*. You notice it and you don't. You know time is passing, but you don't realize that it is also changing—vanishing. Time takes us further away from an answer, not closer. And it is this impasse that makes the Zodiac case, a stand-in for the stalemate of late-stage capitalist existence, unsolvable and chronic.

83. In one key scene, Toschi tells Graysmith, "Zodiac is my job. It is not yours."

While Fincher's use of time stamps has always had a very strong effect on my experience of the film, it was only when I studied the number of time stamps carefully for this essay in the summer of 2019, that I noticed their true intricacy and frequency. Just as analog time-jumps in *Broadcast News* and *The Way We Were* fail to produce a solution to the gender conflict at the center of both films, Fincher's excessive time stamps turn into digital time codes that map out an increasingly untrackable universe of crime.[84] Time is everywhere in *Zodiac*, but corruption is the true clock of the new world.

Nearly every exterior shot in *Zodiac* is digitally altered in some way to be period accurate. Ironically, Fincher achieves this through CGI. Using the non-material of the future, he recuts and digitizes the past.[85] Time becomes a special effect, and the Zodiac Killer the psychosexual

84. James Ellroy's obsessive memoir *My Dark Places* employs a similar technique of detail.

85. Although Ruffalo turns his back to look behind him in the Washington & Cherry murder scene, these scenes were digitally recreated using a green screen, meaning that Ruffalo is actually looking to the digital future. The future of cinema is also the future of time. When time is CG'd, lived time becomes unbearable. At the end of the scene, Toschi steps back to see if the lighting

hard drive of a bygone era. In his review of the film, Seitz writes that "*Zodiac* moves with familiar rhythms, but looks eerily new." As a result of not shooting on film, Fincher's number of takes doubled: in *Fight Club*, released in 1999, Edward Norton claims the average number of takes was 35. In *Zodiac*, released in 2007, Mark Ruffalo claims it was 80 in some cases. In 2019, Jake Gyllenhaal observed, "In the digital world, you can roll for a very long time." In 2019, Benicio del Toro told Michael Douglas (who stars in the Netflix streaming series *The Kominsky Method* and Fincher's *The Game* (1997)), "I started taking my time when digital came in." In *Ways of Hearing*, Krukowski writes that "On tape, there was no 'undo.' You could try again, if you had time and money. But you couldn't move backwards … In the digital studio, everything you do is provisional … There's no commitment, because each element of a recording can be endlessly changed …" Fincher explains that digital footage allows him to look at "hourlies" instead of "dailies." A day's work is collapsed into endless bit takes. 24 frames of truth per second becomes 24 hours of shooting, viewing, posting, sharing, and deleting. Krukowski states: "The digital era has not just altered our tools for working with sound—or image, or moving images. It is changing our relationship to time itself."

is different from where the cab is parked. Fincher states that, "San Francisco is almost a character in the movie." The film's opening shot of San Francisco is a complete CG shot. SF is constantly being referenced and yet many of the scenes were shot elsewhere and/or digitally created.

PART VI: DATES

"It's easier to remember a gesture or a laugh than a date."
—Gilles Deleuze, *Negotiations*

Melanie Graysmith's final on-screen jab to her ex-husband, Robert Graysmith, "It was just the date that never ended," is the affective, digital equivalent of *Zodiac*'s procedural purgatory. A 10-year search for a killer that amounts to nothing[86] is analogous to a marriage that should never have happened. However, read with the passage of time in mind, which is the movie's procedural economy, Melanie's statement is actually about time, not about her relationship with her husband. The word "date" has a double meaning here. Graysmith tells his ex-wife, "Nothing makes sense anymore," a lament that relies on time (one needs time to come to a conclusion about loss and the disintegration of meaning) but does not have a clear object. What is Graysmith actually referring to when he says this? What is nothing? What has changed? What is no more? And what (besides this unsolvable, sprawling mystery that has taken over his life, as evidenced by all the Zodiac research—"crap," as Melanie puts it—that physically surrounds him, consuming his entire apartment) has him on his knees on the living room floor? Melanie's response, "It was just

[86] As actor Mark Ruffalo puts it about the Zodiac, "They don't catch the guy." Ruffalo also appropriately referred to the Zodiac investigation as "sprawling."

the date that didn't end," is what gives Graysmith's ambivalent requiem away. He pretends the lack of "sense" pertains to his marriage; or he is willing to let his ex-wife's dismissal *include* his marriage; serving as a stand-in for the loss of his marriage, if need be, but only by some vague melancholic association. Only if Melanie doesn't push for the actual meaning. Only if we accept that the de facto scene is about a marriage that has ended. Upon further examination, however, we discover that Graysmith's grief is actually about the investigation. And in that sense, *nothing* has changed, as he has only ever been interested in the case, making Melanie and his children one of its (his) casualties. The open-ended loss conjured here is only about Melanie if we—she—presumes it is.

Melanie's use of the word "date" refers to the day she and Robert met—the date that never ended. But unlike all the Zodiac dates, their date (double meaning) wasn't special. "Date" also refers to a movie that is obsessed with dates and built on dates. A movie that was released the same year as the iPhone, another seminal date. A movie in which dates do not add up or lead anywhere, like this marriage; like this case. Like present shock. None of the dates or "hourlies"—the ones Fincher has clocked for nearly three hours—have brought us any closer to the day that we might know who the real Zodiac Killer is. As in, they did not help solve the unsolved mystery. "An epic film about unknowability; defined by unknowing and doubt," observes crime writer James Ellroy in the film's commentary, *Zodiac* is simply *the mystery* that never ended, a mystery into which Melanie got roped.[87] A mystery that consumes Graysmith and that he misunderstands by thinking he alone can find an answer to it. A mystery Graysmith wants so badly to solve he begins a romantic relationship he had no real interest in.[88]

For Fincher and Ellroy, the obsessive tracking of time, along with the crime genre, is a stand-in for failed mourning. Fincher notes that Graysmith has no insight into his own obsession, a pathology that links all men, whether they are criminals or not. He feels "trapped in wanting to know something, and [doesn't] even know if the thing that [he wants] to know is the thing that will finally release [him]." The 1958 murder of Ellroy's mother was famously never solved either. Loss is dumped into an immersive and melancholic investigation that is called male detective work. Ellroy, who in his memoir, *My Dark Places*, admits that he himself was on the path to psychopathy, writes that the crime genre: "was a literary formula preordained directly for *me*. It let me remember and forget in equal measure."

87. Jake Gyllenhaal, who plays Robert Graysmith, calls *Zodiac* "a movie of dead ends."

88. In her essay on *Zodiac* for Criterion, "Fatal Attraction: Women on the Serial-Killer Movies That Thrill Them," Nov 17, 2021, Megan Abbott observes but does not explicitly name the male melancholia ("virus") that haunts the film: "In its final, shattering moments, the movie teeters perilously close to a solution, a confirmation. But Fincher is after a far deeper truth than identifying a killer. Solving the crime would provide momentary satisfaction, but the void it would create is too terrifying to ponder. Obsession—perpetual, inexhaustible—keeps alive the possibility of a deeper logic, a sane world, satisfying answers, closure. On some level, you don't really want to know the truth, because if you did, it would be over and you'd have to face a larger truth—that

the darkness isn't just out there, and spreading. It's inside you. And you've been spreading it, everywhere." On a similar note, in a 2019 email about our mutual love of and obsession with *Zodiac*, writer angelicismo1 asks: "One thing I wonder about is your focus on [Mark] Ruffalo: one could put this philosophically and say why Toschi before Avery and Graysmith?; why not all three as a set or symptom even— the Toschi-Avery-Graysmith symptom; all of them at the same time, or according to phases?... In what sense is Holden [in *Mindhunter*] needed after Graysmith-Avery-Toschi?" For me, the three men of *Zodiac* are a triptych, conglomerate, and progression, like the three men of *Jaws*. They are not so much stages, as phases. I think Toschi is the film's time element. He is the toll. That is why he has that devastating look on his face in the diner at the end of the movie. Toschi conveys the psychic cost. The other men are in the throws of their Zodiac obsession and therefore cannot see clearly. Toschi represents the cultural vanishing that the Zodiac case symbolizes. In a later email, angelicismo1, having watched my durational film *DECADES: 70s*, returns to our shared interest in *Zodiac* as an archive of melancholic masculinity, and observes: "In any case, I finished the 70s portion of *DECADES*, and in some ways that seems to have been the background for all this, the archive trigger, what set me rethinking about these male toxic assets on the archive. I'm imagining this will be the terrain of *Time Tells*, how the male overplays and underplays its hand on the switchboards when it comes to a certain melancholia, and how that's a civilizational stake right now. In what sense is *DECADES* the sheer repetition *Mindhunter* can't quite do; the empty count of mourning the credit sequence? Why DO you hone in on credits in *DECADES*?... When I watch *DECADES*, I feel located, outside the history of film as such, and in a place where I can measure and hear and place my own (sometimes totalitarian) desire to see and watch everything, the desire, a bit like the serial killer's—to own everything at once. I'm given space to roam in that, but also to see it, to locate the desire itself. I couldn't help notice that Derrida uses the word 'toscin' again and again, just as much as you go back to credits— show credits—and so there is a kind of Toschi-effect. Toschi, who is the toll, literally IS the toll, the toscin, the Tosc(h)in." David Shire also conceptualized his *The Conversation*-sourced score for *Zodiac* around the idea of the triptych, by giving each male character his own instrument: the trumpet for Toschi, the solo piano for Graysmith, and the dissonant strings for the Zodiac killer.

WHAT MAKES A MAN CRAZY ENOUGH TO JOIN THE COPS?

Criminals like cops, they don't bring their shit home.

To search for something later always indicates an earlier loss, Freud writes. For Ellroy, the crime genre novels he is now famous for is a causality for the boyhood loss of his murdered mother, specifically the obsessive writing career it spawned. Correspondingly, the Zodiac Killer stands for the death of the lost city of San Francisco, Fincher's childhood home.[89] The city of mystery and memory that became the city of the dot-com boom is the loss of mystery and memory known as gentrification. San Francisco is the wounded city Fincher lost but can now afford to resuscitate digitally.

Fincher:

> I knew about the murder and I knew about the [Zodiac] letters. I grew up in the Bay Area during this period of time. He was a bogeyman for so long. And then when they stopped talking about him, stopped writing about him, stopped mentioning him, all of the sudden, it was like it had never happened. I do profoundly remember when my family moved away from the Bay Area, looking out at the back window of my parents' car as we drove away from our house, and thinking, "Did they ever catch that Zodiac guy?"

---

89. More recent crime docudramas like Fincher's *Mindhunter* (2018) emphasize that the databasing of crimes changed the perception of crimes as well as the patterns of how crimes were committed. In the criminals' attempts to mislead and confuse the police, both the Zodiac Killer and Ted Bundy's crime patterns made time and technology codependent. Zolfo acknowledges this interdependence in his set designs for *Zodiac*: "We tried to tell several stories with the set dressing in the *Chronicle*. In particular, time changes and technology changes. David [Fincher] wanted not so much for the space to change, but for the way that these people did their jobs to evolve. To subtly show tools that became available as we went through time."

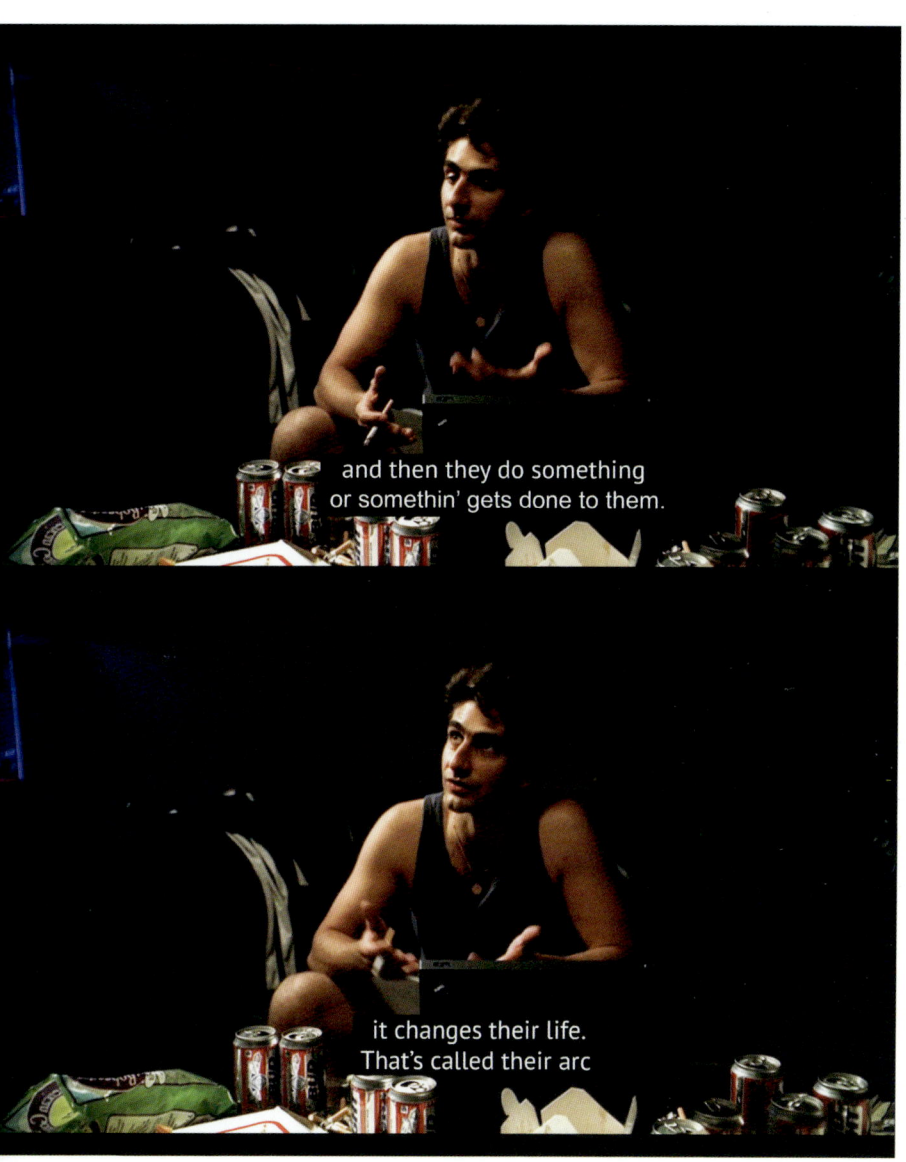

TIME LAG

The 69th Cannes Film Festival Press Conference on *Personal Shopper* featuring Olivier Assayas, Kristen Stewart, and other members of the cast and crew, 2016.

Question: (in French) There's a lot of text messaging, lots of iPhones in the film, why did you choose that specific means of communication? What is your link with technology? Why are you always looking at your telephones?

Olivier Assayas: Well, the text messaging—that shows you how irresponsible I am, in fact. Well, at the outset, one of the avenues I wanted to explore in the film was the following: I wanted to make sort of a little experimental film. A film where the whole of the dialogue would be through text messaging. It's not just a written form of communication. It implies a lot of physical things. A lot of fantasy. And then it struck me as a bit excessive. Yet the idea remained. I wanted to build a film where there would be a whole section with a lot of tension owing to the fact that there was a lot of imaginary communication with someone who was trying to seduce the other person, attract that other person. I wanted to show how one could become captivated and fascinated by what appeared on the screen. These sort of disembodied messengers that kept coming in. Kristin [Stewart] can talk to her relationship with technology and the new means of communication. I believe, however, this is something we all share in one way or another, to differing degrees.

We've become hostage to these means of communication. Sometimes the means of communication end up controlling us. They lay down their modus operandi. It's a bit frightening, it's scary, to see that one can become totally addicted, whether I like it or not. Using a mobile phone, the way I am looking up information on my phone, or communicating with my phone, that's an important part of my life, so it should appear in a contemporary film.

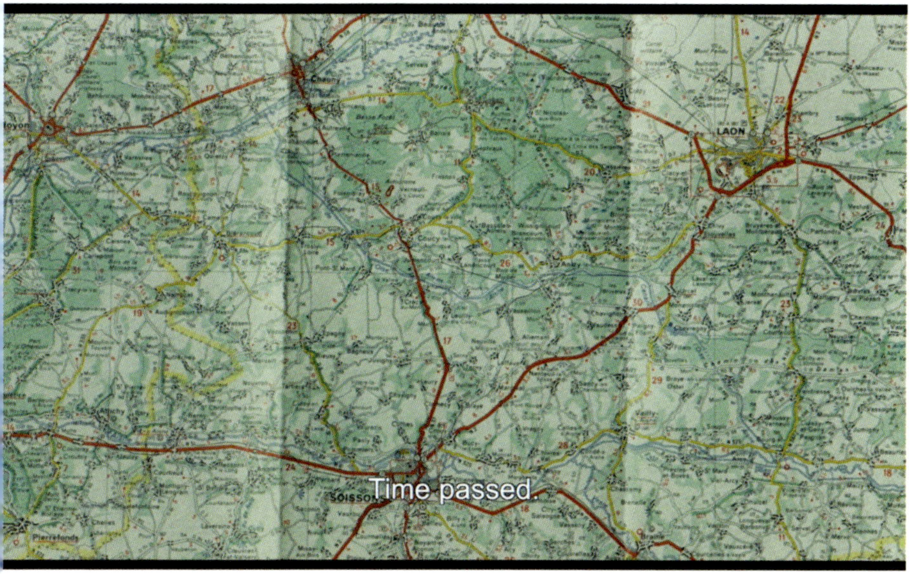
LAON
SOISSO
Time passed.

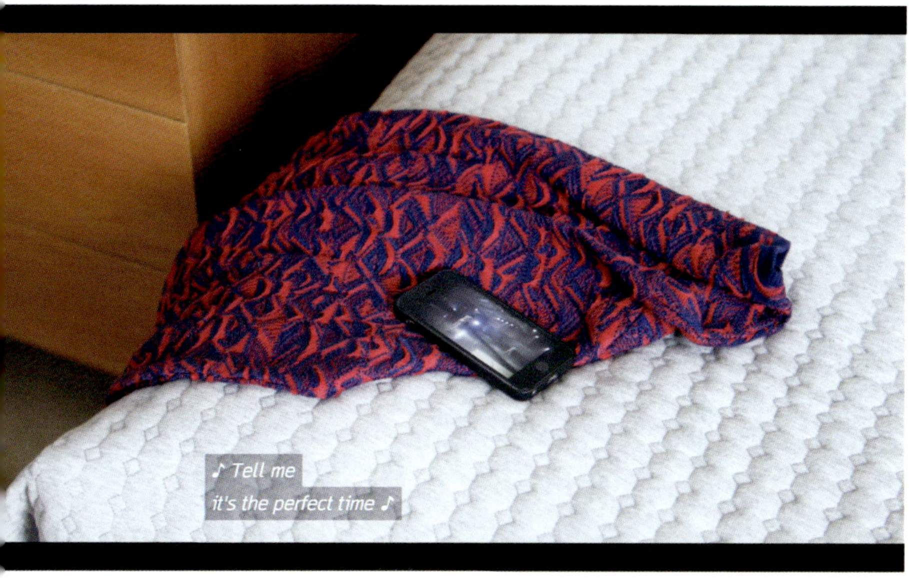
♪ Tell me
it's the perfect time ♪

PAST PERFECT (TOTAL RECALL)

"To create something, it must be based on memories."
—Akira Kurosawa to Chris Marker, 1985

"Only comedy can still get to us" noted the postwar dramatist Friedrich Dürrenmatt. I read this in the Lauren Berlant essay L told me about. This must be what she meant by comedy being the answer.

It is two years later. What is the question now?

The worse things get, the more we laugh. The harder we laugh, the greater the void. We are laughing more than ever. We are laughing all the time.

In August 2018, I spent eight nights re-watching all four seasons of *Felicity*. First on YouTube (whatever I could find) and then a few weeks later on DVDs from start to finish. The rest of the year I watched comedy specials on Netflix and HBO. One every night. Hannah Gadsby's *Nanette*, *Norm MacDonald Has a Show*, Dave Chappelle's three Netflix specials. Chris Rock, Tig Notaro, Louis C. K., Iliza Shlesinger, John Mulaney, Kevin Hart, Hasan Minhaj, Jerrod Carmichael, Samantha B, Amy Schumer, Michael Che, W. Kamau Bell, Michelle Wolf, Ricky Gervais, D. L. Hughley, Hannibal Buress, Sarah Silverman, Katt Williams. Jerry Seinfeld's *Comedians in Cars Getting Coffee*, Aziz Ansari's *Master of None*, Pete Holmes' *Crashing*. I went back to Eddie

Murphy's *Delirious*, 1983. *Richard Pryor: Live in Concert 1979*. Back to George Carlin's *What Am I Doing in New Jersey?*, 1988. Back to Whoopi Goldberg's *The Spook Show*, 1984. Back to *Gilda Radner: Live From New York*, 1979. Lily Tomlin and Richard Pryor's "Juke and Opal," 1973.

Each comedian has a beef. Each beef has a year.

So much of what's funny has to do with what's not.

   "A YouTube video can convince you of anything," jokes Aziz Ansari in his Netflix stand-up, *Right Now*. The 2019 special is damage control for 2018. In it, Ansari tries to convince us that he is still funny after receiving media scrutiny for alleged sexual misconduct at the height of his success. The jokes make up for lost time, but they are also a comedic decoy for the things Ansari wants us to forget.

What is the past doing here? What are we doing with the past?

Does the digital algorithm make everything old or does it make everything, including the past, new?

In doublethink, the past is changeable. Reprogrammable. On YouTube time lives on forever as the present. The past is a digital marketplace. I search for what went wrong, shopping for time.

Everything is a clue. I see things again. I see them for the first time. I see them as I never have. I see them as they never were. The past holds all my questions. The present has no answers.

Paired against the ferocity of the continuous present, the past looks unrecognizable. Big-tech corruption is the new form of time.

Besides skin, what does it mean for something to have been young?

   In the time machine I spend hours studying actors, comedians, writers, musicians, politicians. Time. I watch interviews. I listen closely to the words. I look at the faces, the bodies, the clothes. I realize the camera changes everyone. Changed the world. I realize everyone has changed. Was the camera the first predatory algorithm?

The big world is now in our little pocket. I hit pause. I replay. I look closer. I want to know what I am really seeing. Can we still call what we are seeing today faces? Can we still call people, people? I compare one face to another face. One year to another year. One voice to another voice. One joke to another joke. 1965 to 1979. 2015 to 1988. 1991 to 1958. 2020 to everything else.

I go down the memory hole in order to remember what people were like. To see the difference. To be reminded. I watch people age in reverse. Talk in reverse. I can see what went wrong. I can watch old people grow young. Bad actors turn back into good actors. Bad liars learn to be good liars. I can watch people fear the camera then learn to make eye contact and lie. I watch time make everything worse. Everyone worse. Everyone the same. There she was. There he was. There we were. That place. That city. That year. That decade. That show. That song. That face. That body. Those clothes. That voice. That look. That sound. That time. You could never see it all like this before. All at the same time. Whenever you want.

Every night, I climb into bed and watch everything go back to the way it will never be again.

I can see: What is gone, what has disappeared, what is still left. What is everywhere, what is nowhere.

During the months of lockdown, I wandered the streets of New York City every day for hours. I walked from borough to borough. I walked hundreds of blocks. I finally had the city to myself. The emptiness felt full. Like YouTube, the lockdown gave me time to see, to look, to remember. No one else I knew left their house for months. I couldn't wait to go outside. People ordered their food online while I stood on long lines for mine and cooked every meal. They picked up their delivered boxes. I carried my grocery bags by foot.

In 2020, pandemic distress calls around the subject of pre-internet music began to flood YouTube, where most people appeared to be spending their COVID quarantine. The virus made some people want to remember. Some were not even old enough to remember what they said they missed. Millions of virtual SOSs began to circulate in the comment sections.

The internet suddenly sounded like a radio dispatch in the middle of the ocean:

"It's 2020, anyone else watching this?"

"Anybody listening in 2020?"

Before 2020, I never read YouTube comments. Now I sift through them, looking for answers. Proof that it was real?

Some of the remarks about time—about the world—are more insightful than anything the so-called professional critics have to say. In 2020, people of all ages and time zones set off on a quest. They listened to old songs and watched old music concerts. Each viewer obsessively logs their arrivals, departures, ages, birthdays, dates. Everyone was suddenly commenting on lost time.

"Time is different now," one person claimed. "Within one second of watching this video and listening to their music, my youth has come back," another chimed.

In 2020, everyone wanted to know who else was out there remembering their favorite songs from the pre-cellphone past. Who else was out there thinking about time? Who else wished they could go back? Who else thought that memory is the only real place left to live?

Maybe hope is just another lie the '80s sold to us. But maybe it is a lie that is still true. A lie that wants to be true. What I know is that it felt completely different to be alive then, and that feeling was real. I was happy. A lot of us were. What I love most about music is it says what it means, even if the singer doesn't mean it, or doesn't know how to mean it, or isn't ready to mean it, or isn't allowed to mean it. Music is meaningful in a way that nothing else is meaningful.[90] In 2020, the music of the 20th century opened a portal that made YouTube a virtual bomb shelter for a nonexistent future.

90. In a 2021 interview with the singer Sting about the problem with modern music today, he makes an incredibly important observation: "What I have noticed is that the structure is simpler now. The bridge has disappeared. For me, the bridge is therapy. You set a situation up in a song, like 'My girlfriend left me,' chorus, 'I'm lonely.' You reiterate that again. And then you get to the bridge, and a different chord comes in, and then that viewpoint leads to a key change, and then you realize maybe things aren't so bad. So the bridge is kind of therapy. The structure is therapy. In modern music, most of it, you're in a circular trap; it just goes round and round and round. It fits nicely into the next song and the next song and the next song. But you're not getting that release. That sense that there is a way out of a crisis. And we are in crisis. The world is in crisis…Music needs to show us a way out. And modern music isn't doing that at the moment. I'm looking for solutions [as a musician]. I'm not looking to just reiterate my problem. I want to see how to get out of it. Music can help."

In digital recall, "24 hours of video are uploaded to YouTube every minute," yet the surplus is deceptive.[91] But despite the enormous quantity of videos spanning decades, many things are still missing. Many things about the past are still being ignored. People provide explanations, offer defenses, condolences, fight for their blind spots. I go as far back in time as YouTube will let me to figure out what has changed—in the faces, in the voices, in the clothes. In the words, in the skin, in the eyes. In the music, in the jokes. In the acting.

All the acting on camera is history too.

The past is in trouble. The past is on trial. The past is revenue for a bankrupt present. Things that once belonged to a hidden or forgotten economy are now being unveiled for profit. Some people see nothing, some people see everything.

91. Sameer Padania, in an interview with Adam Phillips, *BOMB*, Issue #113, Oct 1, 2010

What is required in order to see? No one can agree. Time doesn't tell. And if it does tell, we have neither the time nor the heart for what it is showing us.

By the time everything is on YouTube, by which I mean, by the time YouTube exists, everyone knows too many secrets. By which I mean secrets are harder to keep now. By which I mean exposing and talking about secrets has become more profitable than keeping secrets. By which I mean there is money to be made from exposing secrets. By which I mean there is no reason to keep secrets or hide the truth anymore. Time itself is being ransacked and revealed. You can be mad at time forever. You can blame it for everything. It is easier than being angry with or telling the truth about the present. By which I mean time is something we forgot existed until we started pillaging and scrutinizing it on YouTube in 2020. By which I mean if it weren't for all these 24 hours of video every minute, we would still have time to live. A new generation will not be dissuaded from wanting fame and attention. From being on camera. By which I mean fame is a melancholic solution to the erasure of time. By which I mean memory. By which I mean living. By which I mean we might have had a future if we knew how to mourn the past.

"But what program is this, from which I can fashion neither providence nor fate?" Jean-Luc Nancy asks about the transplant science that gives him a new heart in *L'Intrus*.[92]

Before the internet, many lived years were forgotten. By which I mean many years were simply lived rather than watched. Now everything is recalled, yet we remember nothing. By which

92. Discussing her interest in adapting Jean-Luc Nancy's text about his heart transplant for her film of the same name, Claire Denis told Metrograph Theater in 2019: "Men generally always asked the surgeon: Of course, I want a new heart to survive, but not a woman's heart, please. A man, a male heart, not a female heart, please." And an extra demand: "And not from a black person." Clint Eastwood's film *Blood Work*, released in 2002, two years before Denis' film, addresses both of these questions in interesting ways. In the film, Eastwood's FBI agent Terry McCaleb, admits, "I got a new heart. I didn't necessarily get a new life." Unlike Denis' ex-mercenary Louis Trebor, who insists that he wants to keep his "man's character," ex-FBI McCaleb, a white man, not only receives a woman's heart, he receives a Hispanic woman's heart. His transplant is also performed by a female doctor. What,

I mean I miss everything and there is no way to get it back, despite all the videos. Because of all the videos. It is not that "things have changed," as they always have, it is that the things that should never have been tampered with are gone. By which I mean not in us anymore. By which I mean we are no longer capable of living, only watching. YouTube is a software-divination without ontology or foresight.[93] The future today is the rate at which the past can be used to finance the continuous predatory present. A present that ravishes with unrelenting searches, only to ignore what it finds.[94]

What is the past doing here?

the film asks, do we owe to others when they literally give us their hearts? What do we become due to this indebtedness? On whom does our surviving depend? "I think with this new heart, this guy is missing the most important thing," adds Denis. "Something that really belongs to him. Not his whole heart, this heart that doesn't function anymore, but his own life."

93. When it comes to storing and unveiling the past, YouTube works retroactively to become the consumer-present. Time proves nothing. Searching leads nowhere. Time is simply stored for capital. A YouTube video convinces you of everything, as Ansari notes, which is the same thing as being convinced of nothing. In his 2020 Netflix comedy special, *Zero Fu**ks Given*, Kevin Hart jokes: "Everything's gotta be videoed in this generation. If it's not on video, it never happened." Before the digital age, videotape was testimony. Interviews and performances were simply the recorded past. It did not exist beyond the time it was broadcasted. It belonged to time and to people who knew what to do with it (archivists, libraries, and museums). For example, in *Harold and Lillian: A Hollywood Love Story* (2015), film researcher Lillian Michelson refers to print books as "time machines" she could "dip into" whenever she wanted to go somewhere. Each movie Michelson worked on plunged her into a "different life." Directors Mike Nichols, Francis Ford Coppola, Stanley Kubrick, and David Lynch employed Michelson to "pursue the past." One production designer referred to her famously eclectic basement library at Paramount Studios as an "alchemist's lab." In Michelson's movie archive, time was a form of sorcery and knowledge. She was prized as an expert mixer of time periods, making her database a portal of discovery rather than simply a resource for historical pastiche. Her film library had a "rather unusual filing system … space and religion [were] next to each other because they both belonged in the heavens." Michelson says she learned the most from the research she did on witchcraft for *Rosemary's Baby* and on birds for Hitchcock's titular film. Thus, if the essence of technology, which is to say, its unfolding—its evolution—was destined long before it appeared during the Industrial Revolution; that is, if technology is and always was our destiny, as Heidegger writes in the 1953 lecture, "The Question Concerning Technology" (originally called "The Enframing"), does it already take into account our responses to it; foretelling our losses as well as our future servitude? For example, is the public display of our memory of musical time a human glitch? Or does technology take these analytics into account ahead of time, simply allowing us to access our losses in the form of an already-prepared algorithm? Our losses lead us to data-losses. In his introduction to Heidegger's essay, David Farrell Krell writes that technology does not forsake the course of human destiny, but in fact, was destined to be sent to us long before the eighteenth

century. In other words, technology did not begin chronologically.

94. In 1985, Akira Kurosawa told Chris Marker: "To create something it must be based on memories." YouTube can be thought of as the misuse and mishandling of the oracle, a metagaming of the past. In 2020, YouTube astrologer, Acyuta-bhava Das (aka Adam Elenbaas) offers the following warning about the study of ancient astrology (now popularized due to the explosion of astrology on the internet) as divination: "Any form of divination requires sacrifice … The idea is that you have to have some skin in the game with your ancient astrology. You can't just sort of show up and say, 'Give me some answer. I want it.' That selfish kind of interest is frowned upon by the gods who are the mouth pieces of the Oracle. They speak on behalf of godhead. So when you're approaching the Oracle and you don't have some sense of sacrifice of your own will, of your own ego, of your own selfish interest, you're a lot less likely to develop a healthy relationship with the oracle." Similarly, we cannot simply exploit online video-sharing platforms like YouTube in order to incite the imperative: "Show me the past."

What kind of failed mourning is YouTube? What kind of chronological scheme? What is the past doing here?

I watch old interviews on YouTube and read the comments afterwards, I understand two paradoxical things at once: whatever was left of the world was still here and whatever was left of the world is now gone.

The twentieth century was the century of acting. Of learning to live on camera. This lesson was for all of us. The lesson was for life. The movie actors trained us. The project of the second decade of the twenty-first century is to cancel the project of the twentieth century. Every day we learn about what people of the twentieth century and twenty-first century did wrong. What they are really like (now) and also what they never really were (then). What they pretended to be. How they fooled us. How we wanted to be fooled. How they still fool us while pretending not to anymore. How we now have the tools to fool them back. The second decade of the twenty-first century is a giant algorithm of the twentieth century. How much did we gain by not wanting to know for so many years? How much do we lose by wanting to know everything now? Everything the twentieth century taught us the world should be, we are now told was a form of deception and violence.[94] Which makes all of us victims of what? The twenty-first century? Modernity? Progress? Ourselves? By which I mean, was it the wrong kind of world or are we the wrong kind of people?

The economy of constant exposure is the highest form of cover up.

---

94. "What attitudes would our culture have to sacrifice to imagine a better one?" asks Alexis Soloski. "Woody Allen, Mia Farrow and What Popular Culture Wants to Believe," The *New York Times*, March 2, 2021. In a 2021 *Vanity Fair* feature on the history of Hammer men and the Armie Hammer allegations, "The Fall of Armie Hammer: A Family Saga of Sex, Money, Drugs, and Betrayal," Julie Miller, makes a generational distinction that could also be used to distinguish between the twentieth and twenty-first centuries: "Armie may not be the first Hammer accused of darkness, but he could be the first to suffer public consequences…Those who know Armie professionally have had a hard time watching the Armie they knew seemingly implode in a fit of social media posts, bad behavior, and substance abuse in recent months (Though how would Armie's namesake, Armand, have fared in a social media

YOU'RE STILL ADDICTED TO THE 20th CENTURY,

How do we hate the kind of people we are still being taught to worship? How do we worship the people we are now taught to blame? What do we do with all the crimes being revealed? With the algorithms of the past? With the people whose careers and fortunes and lies we make possible and cannot live without? With a constant present that cancels any meaningful assessment by leaving no time for thinking? How can I mourn a century and also miss it? How can I tell who is good if everyone is revealed to be bad? What does it take to be good when everything is bad? The late twentieth century and early twenty-first invented techniques to map and decode an astonishing web of crimes, but in doing so we have created an even more intricate criminal syndicate called the Future. Knowing about injustice replaces not knowing about injustice. Exposing injustice replaces the concealing of injustice. Deception is reengineered as a preprogrammed world?)." In 2016, the writer Jarett Kobek told *LitHub*, "There's no way to write about the Internet without writing about celebrity." Conversely, there is no way to talk about viruses and corruption, memory and loss, without talking about celebrity in the social media age. In *The Devil's Advocate* (1997), the Devil takes credit for the twentieth century, telling his son: "Who, in their right mind, could possibly deny the twentieth century was entirely mine? … Millennium's comin', title fight."

algorithm encrypted for a mediated outcome and reaction. Does our constant media reckoning with the crimes and misdemeanors of the past buy us time for the more unfathomable and unsolvable crimes that are coming? That are here?

On finding new reasons to live after he receives his heart transplant, Nancy concludes, "Why always revert back to asymptote of an absence of suffering? An old question, but one whose stakes are raised by technology to a height which, it must be admitted, we are far from ready."

Everyone I have ever talked to insists that nothing ever really changes. That change always happens in the exact same way. But now, there is only change. Change has never been this fast or this constant. Change is destroying everything we have ever known. The difficulty is what to make of all the changes, which amounts to too many losses. How to understand what we are seeing when there is no time to see what we are seeing. No time to change. No time to think. No time to understand or mourn all that we did wrong. If, in its essence, modern technology is revealing, the only way left of revealing beings, and the only way human beings are capable of revealing themselves, what happens to revealing—to its value, to its autonomy, to its power? How do we live with all the seeing? The seeing of everything that is being revealed? The seeing of everything that has been destroyed. The seeing of everything that is wrong. The seeing that has replaced living. How to keep up with all the changing? With the threat of being left behind. With the promise of going forward when there is nowhere left to go. How to change. How to pay attention. How to not pay attention. How to turn away. Where would you go? This is not the same thing as being distracted. It is the opposite of being distracted. When there is too much information; when all the old crimes are mixed in with the new crimes; the good people are mixed in with the bad; pleasure is mixed in with entertainment, outrage, self-promotion, and cancellation; money becomes bankruptcy; loss is gain; success is failure. The future is ruin. The concealment of crimes and the exposure of crimes one and the same. Continuous and constant. We are left with only two choices now: pay attention less or pay attention more. Pay attention to everything or pay attention to nothing. Life or death of life. "The internet is forever,"[95] but so is—we are learning—our insatiable need for loss. The old idols are the new monsters. The new idols are proof the old monsters can never go away.

What is the past doing here?

95. Elizabeth Chambers on her ex-husband Armie Hammer and his infamous cannibalistic sex DMs.

PAST PERFECT
(FUTURE NOSTALGIA)

Do you know what happened? Does anyone know what happened? Elon Musk ... sent many, many telecom satellites into the sky that look exactly like stars, exactly like stars. So now when we humans gaze at the night sky, they won't know if they're gazing at a star or at a machine. And we at this table, at this little table, we are among the last, the very last, ever, ever, to have seen the actual, real, the honest, truthful night sky from the ocean. We saw stars. Just stars.

—*Let Them All Talk*, 2020

WHILE WE'RE YOUNG

WARHOL: Do you get depressed if you don't work?
ADAM HOROVITZ: Yes, and I don't want to talk about it.
—Q & Andy, *Interview*, April 7, 2015[96]

In a 2015 *GQ* interview, "The Ad-Rock Retirement Plan," Adam Horovitz, aka Ad-Rock of the Beastie Boys, declared that he had missed out. It had been three years since the founding member of the band, Adam Yauch, died of cancer at 47, and Horovitz was still in mourning. After a lifetime of playing music and touring around the world, he ended the band and settled down at home. He had lost Yauch, he had lost his band, he had even lost some time. Horovitz was a teenager when his mother, Doris Keefe, died from alcoholism. Dodging his first real encounter with grief and loss, he escaped into music and fame. He had no time to mourn. He made no time.

At 53, with Yauch gone, and no band, Horovitz has nowhere to hide. With "too much time on his hands," he is trying to make up for

96. Adam Horovitz, who has one of my favorite faces of all time, has pulled many faces in his career: Elvis, Billy Idol, Pee-wee Herman, and Robert De Niro were all part of his repertoire when he was young.

lost time by going back in time, where it is always still the '90s.

GQ writes:

> [Adam Horowitz] and Kathleen [Hanna] play Scrabble. They spend a lot of time "watching judge shows and eating pizza," Adam says. Back in the '90s, he missed out on a ton of popular culture—was too busy touring, making music, being pop culture. "I didn't watch *Seinfeld*, *Simpsons*; I didn't watch any of that shit when it was out." So he's been catching up. Smoking weed, smoking ribs, watching the Knicks.

The *N.Y. Times* refers to Horovitz as "A Beastie in Middle Age." *Pitchfork* asks, "Beastie Boys: What Happened?" Another article is titled, "Death, Celebrity, and Fatherhood." In every interview after Yauch's death, Horovitz and Mike Diamond, aka Mike D, the other surviving member of the musical trio, are reminded that they are getting old. Every question leads to death.

What is too late? Who is too old? What is gone?

It is shocking to hear men being talked to and written about this way. Horovitz and Diamond represent a bygone era—the 1990s. The constant focus on their age masks a cultural loss. Time has passed. Things have changed.[97]

When a body ages, or hasn't aged enough, we lose our rights to certain experiences, certain

---

97. When bands start making bad music, the clock of mortality is always evoked. Something has gone wrong that cannot be reversed. In 2006, Mark Richardson wrote in *Pitchfork*, "Considering the dramatic shift in my interest in all things Beastie Boys circa 1995, and then my feeling by the time they got around to releasing *Hello Nasty*, you'd think I had some sort of brush with death or life-altering epiphany in between. Somehow, they'd lost all relevance to me, and it was apparent from listening to the record once. I don't know if they'd 'lost it' or if I moved on and I still don't … there was no turning back … What changed? Had people my age gone over our little pop culture history with such detail at that point that there was nothing left to say?" This question seems especially relevant in the age of social media where every detail of young performers and viewers reactions

times and places. Horovitz says he knows and accepts this, an unusual admission for a man with his success. Horovitz says hip-hop is "full of midlife crisis." Has his feminist wife, the Riot grrrl singer Kathleen Hanna, taught Horovitz about the privilege of time? Has she taught him that time plays a role, even for—*especially* for—men?

But the Beastie Boys aren't just aging; they are time capsules of an era that has aged out of favor. Horovitz, once a foremost culture-maker, has ironically missed out on all the time he was busy making. It is time now, he says, to stay put.

to them is publicly expressed and on display from the get-go.

Time to stop.

To Jonathan

27

THERE IS STILL TIME...

"What am I going to do?" Horovitz asks on the podcast *Sway's Universe*. "Listen to *new* songs? When you become an old person, you get stuck in a different time period ... The kids today don't give a shit what I think. And that's how it should be ... Chuck D [of Public Enemy] is not trying to be twenty years old ... Old people old. Young people young."

Horovitz's surprising answer undercuts a question that is normally taken for granted. A question that men are not normally even asked. Diamond, less reflective, provides a more conventional answer, telling George Strombo in 2018 that he never looks back. "I am almost anti-reflective ... I'm a move-forward type of dude." Horovitz nods in agreement. "He is. It's *annoying* ... Mike uses it to get out of arguments a lot. 'I don't deal in the past,' he always tells me, 'I move forward.'"

Normally only women's worth is assessed in relation to time. Women are deemed too old to be anything unless they are deemed girls, reduced to what Marguerite Duras called "children *for nothing*." The world goes to the perpetual boy, who inherits the earth. To ask a man, *what are you without your work?* is not a question ever posed to women. To ask a man what he does if he is not working, is to ask him what he does when he is at home, where women are expected to be, where the feminine lives and waits, where others must be cared for, where time is forced to exist. It is to ask him what else he could possibly have to live for? What else could possibly have value for him? It is to ask him if he loves anything other than himself.

But why is Horowitz's and Diamond's age so important to the press? Why was it discussed in every article that is published after Yauch's death? Horovitz and Diamond are constantly being asked if they are afraid to die; if they miss Yauch; if they know they are getting old; if they know their hair has turned gray;[98] if they worry about what to do with the rest of their lives. If they know they too are vulnerable to time. "*Ill Communication*," reminisces Horovitz in the *Beastie Boys Book*, "came from us being obsessed with being together and making music." Horovitz, who is thought of as the physical clown in a group that was always three-part comedy troupe[98]—"the 3 Stooges of Rap"—and who has become a dramatic actor since the band ended, claims he doesn't know what to do with his time. But he has always claimed this, even when he was young and said he didn't expect to live past the age of 25.

Diamond says this isn't true. "Adam makes it sound like he does nothing. But he's on a caffeine-fueled rampage at 6:30 a.m. with his emails." "First thing in the morning, boom. Get it done. Boom, boom, boom. After that, I like to hang out," Horovitz jokes. When an interviewer in 1996 asked, "Do you ever think of retiring?" Horovitz, about to turn 40, answered, "I don't really work anyway, so why retire? [laughs]."

When one died, all three died.

There is Yauch's death; there is our death. There is the death of a culture and time, dredged up and pined for through the flashback of a song. When we pose these vicarious questions about other people's deaths, other people's ages, other people's time, "are we taking in the spectacle of our own lost innocence?" Claire Dederer asks in her essay on art made by monstrous men. If the Beastie Boys are "old" and tired now, it is because the '90s are so far away.[100] It is because time has gotten too old to keep acting so young. How can we forgive Horovitz and Diamond for losing time if we can't forgive ourselves for throwing the world away? How can we let go of lost time, if these "old" men are not willing to continue acting young?

Yauch's death freezes them. Now they can't pretend. Now they have to stop. Now boyhood ends. Now time stands still.

Diamond only looks forward. Horovitz has always looked back, afraid of the death ahead.

98. In *Check Your Head*, Mike D humorously prophesizes: "And I can rock a block party / 'til your hair turns gray."

99. According to the band, part of the early project of the Beastie Boys was to parody and impersonate the worst excesses of frat-boy masculinity. In the 1980s, during their first tour, the British tabloids referred to the group, as a "traveling circus." Visual artist and friend, Cey Adams, says the Beastie Boys spent a lot of time laughing, both as a musical group and as friends. In nearly all of the '80s and '90s interviews I have watched, the Beastie Boys are in character—joking, stoned. Their answers to questions are nearly always gags: fictional, silly, absurd. They avoid any kind of promotional or straightforward press script, opting for rock 'n' roll theater instead. Horovitz often refused to talk at all during interviews, zoning

In a 2014 *N.Y. Times* profile on Mike D's townhouse in Brooklyn's Clinton Hill, the rapper, along with his ex-wife, the filmmaker Tamra Jenkins, is disparaged for concealing his age. He says he'd rather not have it in print. He is called vain, as a woman might be called. In a 2018 hour-long podcast with George Strombo about the Beastie Boys' band memoir, *Beastie Boys Book*, YouTube comments focus on Diamond's "hanging skin," his "vagina neck." Horovitz's gray hair ("I wish I had better hair. I wish I were a little taller," he told *N.Y. Times* in 2020). They are evaluated and ridiculed physically, despised for getting older. In the home profile of Diamond, the *N.Y. Times* writer chastizes that anyone can easily find Diamond's age online. So what is he hiding by not revealing a number everyone already knows? By not acknowledging that decades and albums logically add up to trackable years? He cannot be younger than all the years of *music*. He cannot erase all the times he's already cited his age in interviews. Even if he "never looks back," surely, he must know that. Diamond is treated like a woman who is terrified of aging.

The recession of a culturally-thriving era of twentieth century white American masculinity—young, brash, independent, comic, visionary—feminizes them. Were it not for that culture expiring and dissolving, the Beastie Boys could have lived on as ageless stage men—ushering themselves into a new era, untethered to the past, oblivious of and immune to time; using women—and the stage—to remain eternally young and culturally intact.[102]

But Yauch's death has made this impossible. Feminism has made it impossible too. Through out and making faces instead, while Mike D, the diplomat and negotiator of the group, did most of the talking. They were, as Mike D explains in *The Skills to Pay the Bills*, "dead serious" about the "joke" of *Licensed to Ill* and the questionable behavior that accompanied it. Despite a few half-serious interviews in the second half of the 2000s, this approach to the press went on for most of their career. "Why do people really listen to our music?" Horovitz asks himself in *The Skills to Pay the Bills*. "The only thing I can think of, we think it's really funny." Former drummer for the Beastie Boys, Kate Schellenbach, refers to *Licensed to Ill* as a "comedy record." During the making of their second album, *Paul's Boutique*, the Beastie Boys stayed at the Mondrian Hotel in Los Angeles, across the street from The Comedy Store, a famous comedy club. The band regularly threw eggs at the people waiting

237

Hanna, Horovitz has been especially proximate to the politics of time. By stopping, by disbanding and leaving the musical stage, the Beastie Boys have decided to age." It's like, what do you do with your life when your former life is no more? I have to figure it out. I don't know if I ever will," a now homebound Horovitz told *Rolling Stone* shortly after Yauch passed.

In "Sounds of Science," Yauch predicts the future, chanting, "*I'm gonna die gonna die one day*," as if preparing his other bandmates for what is to come. In "I Don't Know," released in 1998, Yauch describes their future without him:

I don't know
Who does know
Where to go
I don't know
I don't know
I don't know
I don't know

In 1992's "Pass the Mic," Ad-Rock tells us, "I'm always on time, y'all" before passing the mic to Yauch, who cautions, "Tick tock y'all."

The threesome—now two—no longer hold the same value—to us or to themselves—nor do they expect to. Men, in general, no longer hold the same value, even though they expect to. Horovitz and Diamond are more like women now, which means their time is up. Which means they know that men no longer control the story of Time.

on line from their hotel window. John King, from the Dust Brothers, and co-producer of *Paul's Boutique*, describes the album as a record of "inside jokes." "People didn't know how to take them—was this for real? Was it a joke?" says former Beastie Boys manager and Capitol Records president, Andrew Slater. In the *Beastie Boys Book*, Horovitz, remembering Yauch, writes, "Funny is very important." In addition to being funny, Horovitz, is also the only member of the group who dances onstage. Yauch never danced when he performed, Diamond jumped and bobbed. Horovitz shimmied with his whole body.

100. In a 2013 interview with Kathleen Hanna on "The Interview Show," Mark Bazer jokes, "What were the '90s? They're over, right?" In the rap song, "They Reminisce Over You," Pete Rock & CL

Smooth sing, "I reminisce so you never forget this / My God, it's so / so lovely / That's how we like to do it in the '90s."

101. In 2017, a 55-year-old Dave Gahan, front man for Depeche Mode, told Kate Mossman at the *New Statesman*, "The stage is the only place where I don't feel my age."

102. The only article I have read in which the interviewer focuses on Diamond and Horowitz's "youthfulness" (Horovitz's humor and goofiness in particular), rather than their aging, was in *The Observer*. Interestingly, the article was written by a woman. On the podcast *Sway's Universe*, Heather B. Gardner commends Horowitz for his honesty about aging: "Nobody is bold enough to say what you're saying. People come up here and they tap dance and they want everybody to be their friend, and they need the next new young thing to be on their record. So they won't say that. They don't wanna be the old person. They don't even want to recognize their age. So for you to say it… it's good to hear you say it." When Sway jokingly tells Horovitz that he is going to take his Beastie Boy stripe off of him, Horovitz irreverently replies with, "Go ahead." On the trio's much beloved '90s song, "Sabotage," which Horowitz famously screams, he reflects, "Why am I yelling? Take it down a notch." Horovitz's other thoughtful jabs at himself about time and aging on the podcast include quips like, "Apps? What am I, 12?"

239

2014 (THE AGE OF STYLE)

"If I could design time, that would be very nice."
—Yohji Yamamoto, 1988

PART I

Masha Tupitsyn: Let's start by talking about your unique and special upbringing. All the women in your family were artists, seamstresses, and knitters, so art and clothing were fused early on. For a long time, both your mother and aunt made clothes for you. Was this purely because you didn't have money to buy the clothes you liked? Did you design them together? When I look at some of those clothes now in photographs, I think of them not simply as articles of clothing, or even examples of innovative style, but as art objects. And I still wear a lot of those pieces myself because they've lasted. Where do you think style comes from? Where does yours?

Margarita Tupitsyn: Most Russians were really poor, so they couldn't afford to wear the high fashions of the West. But there was also simply nothing to buy in the department stores. The only people who dressed well were people who had access to the West or who made their own clothes. On rare occasions, things were brought from abroad and people would stand on these long, horrible lines to buy something. And most people didn't have any money anyway. In my case, my mother, grandmother, and aunt compensated for that absence by making basic things for my family and me to wear. My aunt, the painter Lydia Masterkova, was a different story, however. She could sew, but that was not her primary vocation or interest. She was an abstract artist, and therefore had an avant-garde approach to form and could make anything—clothes, jewelry, furniture. If we think of the history of the Russian avant-garde in the 1920s, where design played a dominant role, often even overshadowing painting, my aunt was steeped in this tradition. She also liked to dress me in vintage clothes dating as far back as the nineteenth century. She loved Fellini's *La Strada*, which was a big hit in Russia in the 1960s, and would style me as Gelsomina, played by the actress Giulietta Masina. Lydia gave me all these identities and characters through clothing. Of course she also made clothes for herself and was always amazingly dressed. She was a feminist, which she, funnily enough, also expressed through clothes. Married to the abstract painter, Vladimir Nemukhin, she had this rule that whenever he needed his shirts ironed for some important party, she would only iron what you could see! She wouldn't bother to iron the part of the shirt that was hidden underneath the jacket, like the sleeves. So my aesthetic sensibility came from my aunt and uncle, who collected antiques and had completely unusual and atypical objects in their homes. They showed me beautiful art history books with amazing Renaissance paintings.

Lydia Masterkova and Vladimir Nemukhin, Moscow, 1959

Masha: So what role did fashion play in the Russian avant-garde of the 1920s, and how did it influence artists like your aunt and uncle later on?

Margarita: Russian avant-garde artists believed that fashion should be egalitarian, part of everyone's life and that all things should be beautiful and aestheticized. They were against fashion as elitist. Artistic creativity was a way to realize the utopia of beauty and refinement. But after Stalin's regime of violent repression and unprecedented austerity, this sensibility was lost as a social standard. My aunt subscribed to this ethos of aesthetic cohherence because she could make things herself and because she had this incredible eye. She believed one's *whole* environment should be cultivated. And, of course, rich people had always pursued this idea of the total environment—the difference being much of this luxury was economically driven. But for my aunt it was part of this artistic, bohemian ideal.

Lydia Masterkova, Priluki, Russia, 1967

Masha: We know that people can be very interested in aesthetics in a way that is compartmentalized. For example, they might go to a museum to appreciate art, but have no interest in clothes or in surrounding themselves with so-called beautiful objects. Or, they might decorate their homes but not their faces or bodies—so very heightened and cultivated aesthetics in one area and inactive aesthetics in another.

Now, of course, with the prominence of the nouveau riche model of insta-fame and wealth that entertainment culture has made more visible, this idea of refinement and deep style has been further degraded because there is rarely a personally fostered relationship to aesthetics over time. Now we have a consumer mentality. Wealth is composed of cheap status signifiers you can purchase anywhere. You have no idea what you're buying, or why—only that it is "expensive" and brand driven, even when it's fake. Before, wealth had everything to do with worth, taste, and exclusivity. When you had something beautiful, however corrupt it was to acquire that beauty—and it's always been corrupt—you had it because you knew having it *meant* something. Wealth and beauty are not about what lasts anymore, or where something comes from, or even what it means to you. New equals value. Upgrading reigns supreme. It's the gaudy cost of things we're seeing, not the value.

Margarita: The '50s, '60s, '70s art world in Europe and America, but also more generally too, could not afford the clothes that movie figures like Audrey Hepburn or Jackie Onassis were wearing. The art world was poor, so art and glamour were still separate and distinct. The '60s can be compared to the 1920s avant-garde because the '60s were a rebirth of those incredibly innovative ideas—the notion of *all-around* elegance. The art bohemia of the '70s boycotted glamour; they did not stake their identity in clothing. Artists were doing conceptual things. It was about the dematerialization of an object, dematerialization of clothing, the politicization of everyday life. So decorative and aesthetic indulgences just didn't matter to them. And then in the '80s, it changed again. Clothing became synonymous, as you point out in your essay, "Mixed Signals" on *Pretty in Pink* (1986), with identity. It mattered. If you wanted to be visible, you *had* to dress in an interesting and radical way. You had to communicate your ideas through dress. People in the art world started to pay attention to how people were dressed and that's when Japanese avant-garde designers like Comme des Garçons, Yohji Yamamoto, and Issey Miyake appeared. In the mid-'80s, my style changed drastically. Before that, my mother had been sewing patterns based on designers like Valentino and Dior for me to wear, and while some of those clothes were beautiful, they never really suited my sensibility, and my husband, Victor Tupitsyn, who has an incredible eye, knew that even before I did.

In 1984, I bought a pair of shoes at a department store on 57th street in New York, without knowing they were CDG. And then later, I was walking through Soho one day, in 1985, and I saw this totally minimalist store, fashioned out of gray concrete with nothing in it but a few racks of black clothing (CDG's first store in the '80s was on Wooster Street, which opened in 1983), and I looked at the clothes and felt the way I did during my childhood—that clothing is art rather than something you simply cover or gender your body with. The clothes reminded me of what my aunt was making as far as formal invention is concerned. I could hardly believe it, and from that point on, I was stuck on Japanese designers.

Masha: There is a moment in Wim Wenders' film on Yohji Yamamoto, *Notebook on Cities and Clothes* (1989), where Wenders remarks that when he put on Yamamoto's clothes "something was different." Right away, Wenders says the clothes felt new and old at the same time. "I was wearing the shirt itself and the jacket itself. And in them, I was myself. I felt protected like a knight in his armor." This made me think of your interest in Japanese clothing in the '80s and also how I learned to wear clothes from you. This idea—of something feeling new and old at the same time—has always been my favorite quality in art, as well as people. The idea of honoring tradition while breaking new ground. There is another moment in the film when Yamamoto looks through August Sanders' *People of the 20th Century*, a book both he and Wenders love, and observes that the people have "exactly the right faces and clothes. Their clothes clearly represent their business and their life." Yamamoto is referring to a kind of perfect harmony and synergy between form and content. What Wenders calls "a craftsman's morals." Not the total arbitrariness of today, where you can't tell anything about anyone. Clothes, much less behavior, aren't meant to signify anything coherent, revealing, or cohesive about someone. Of course, this might seem like a contradiction given Yamamoto's love of asymmetry. But asymmetry, he says, is the mark of the *human* touch. "We have to make the true chair, true jacket, true shirt." Yamamoto goes even further, suggesting that there should be an apprenticeship for teaching these morals, in order to pass them down. To endow others with *moral skills*. I love the idea of moral or honest clothes. "Not consuming clothing, but living with clothes," as Yamamoto says. It's a very beautiful idea, especially given how corporate and corrupt the fashion industry is now. It also makes me think of the saying, "The clothes make the man," which is backwards. It's the *person* that makes the clothes. This is the definition of style, I think.

All this to say, I can vividly remember you picking me up from school wearing your first CDG ensemble. I was maybe seven and everyone was staring at you and I couldn't figure out why. Suddenly you dressed differently and your hair was gone. I think you had just cut all your hair off. This was the age of big, long hair and bright colors and shoulder pads, and you were dressed in spartan black and looked like a boy. The clothing really confused your gender and perplexed everyone. Everyone at school, or even the supermarket, would ask me if you were my brother. I could tell how much those clothes excited you. It was a total shift, but also an organic one. However, while you discovered your style utopia, I also felt that the power and radicality of what you were wearing, and its effect on others, was profound. And yet, I never felt embarrassed by you. I always felt pride. I knew, somehow, that those choices and gestures were an essential part of your individuality and thinking, and that it would be to mine as well. I also remember having postcards of Christy Turlington wearing CDG and how unadorned and laconic those early fashion ads were. Like the reality, the ethos, was the clothing, as you said. The clothes were a *state of mind*—a social and intellectual value system. How you *lived*, not just how you *dressed*—a very Zen precept. That's why there is nothing else in the background of these ads. No commodity-relation or affect, as it were.

Margarita: Yes, there was a mindful austerity and asceticism to these clothes; no accessories, visible makeup, or fashion "scenes." Everything was stripped down to the bare essentials, while in today's consumer economy aesthetics function as pure excess and entertainment proxy. There is also the fact that people essentially stopped paying attention to

Christy Turlington, Comme des Garçons, 1985

avant-garde clothing and avant-garde principles and ideas. I remember when I wore Jean Paul Gaultier in the '80s, who was also radical at the time but in a very different way from Japanese designers, people would stop me on the subway to ask me if I was wearing a costume. The only time I didn't get stopped was on Halloween. There was something powerful and shocking about being outrageous or different. The result was that people were surprised and curious. A lot of this has to do with the problem and proliferation of the copy and of the mass-marketing of "style" in general, which is an effect of mass production and entertainment culture. You can reproduce anything and recirculate it endlessly, both in images and in copy. When you copy something and make it available everywhere, the originality and effect degrades. So again, while that utopian Russian idea of the egalitarianism of design is a great idea, it doesn't really work in consumer culture. When promotional culture tells us where to get high-end designs for cheap, how to recreate high fashion looks, and everything turns to cheap affective labor, we lose the personal value and durability of things. We lose the source—the context—of why and how that clothing functions and why we choose to wear one thing and not another.

Masha: But now we have an additional problem—we have branded and over-styled literally everything, so there is no real individual style anymore and therefore no real thrill in discovering style—a neighborhood, a house—or dressing up. Hence, the proliferation of stylists and decorators everywhere micromanaging and mediating our tastes and interests. If it doesn't result in difference, it's very hard for me to understand the point of wearing something. As much as I love and have always loved clothing—it's in my DNA, as it were—style for me is fiercely personal. It is about discovery and finding your *own* look. I learned that from you. Now everyone knows what's what and who's who and who wore what to what and where to buy it—everything is worn in a very meta and branded way, which has made me feel very ambivalent about the power and value of style. So given this total appropriation, what's the point? I like beautiful and interesting things, but I no longer believe in the power of aesthetics as something *outside* of commodity culture. What are your thoughts on this, especially in the context of art and aesthetics?

Margarita: The worst thing that's happened to our concept of clothing is this all-pervasive concept of sexy, of women having to be uniformly and excessively sexy, which is what Japanese designers defied by de-sexualizing and de-gendering clothing. For them, clothing was about expressing who you are *through* clothing, not simply signaling cues of desirability. The clothes concealed women's bodies and distorted their shape, so that even if you were thin, for example, that wasn't the point. You didn't have to show that you were thin or what your body actually looked like. The clothes were formeless.

Masha: Exactly. You didn't have to parade the body or some ideal of the body. Avant-garde clothes, but even just the voluminous, asymmetrical, baggy, slouching shapes of mainstream '80s clothes, which carried over into the '90s, did not present straightforward representations of the female body. It wasn't some rudimentary outline of tits & ass. Now, if you have large breasts, you have to wear tops that showcase your breasts. If you have what the culture has determined as a "nice" body, you wear form-fitting clothes. And with *Sex and the City*, you must always wear heels now to sexualize and advertise your legs, for example. It's all gone very basic and into this normative direction. That cynicism and commercialization of alternative culture has definitely affected my relation to clothes. It's disenchanted me.

Margarita: I always dressed for myself. Wearing those clothes was a very strong part of my psychology. Of feeling happy, feeling confident. It was not only my uniform; it was extension of my creative and intellectual sensibilities. Your dad always said that I mopped the floor in my best outfits, which means those clothes were not simply about "dressing up," or going out, they were fused with my everyday life. They were practical. Whereas today clothes are trophies and status symbols—it's who's wearing what with what and how much it cost and getting photographed in what you wear to some social event. It's how their body looks. So, while Japanese designers like CDG de-emphasized schisms between everyday life and glamour, rich and poor, inner and outer, male and female, celebrity culture re-emphasizes all these norms and binaries even when they pretend to be dismantling them.

Masha: I used to do that, too—paint or clean my apartment in my best dress. As a result, I ruined a lot of clothes with paint and bleach stains! But, as you say, I just couldn't take those things off because psychologically they were part of me and what I was doing. For me, clothes are internal, not just external. Clothes framed things psychologically and put me into a certain kind of mood.

Why do you think some people lose their style? Does it simply have to do with the individualism, rebellion, experimentation, and aesthetic freedom that sometimes comes with youth? We were talking about Johnny Depp yesterday. How elegant he used to be, along with Winona Ryder, his girlfriend in the early '90s; how their style was part of being anti-style in Hollywood. There was also a default stylishness built into the culture until about the mid-'90s, which meant that a lot of actors, artists, and musicians had style just by virtue of the implicit style embedded into the arts—even the mainstream arts—at that time. I see that with bands all the time. You can always check whether someone has true style by how they look and dress after the culture *at large* degraded after the mid-90s. Case in point, Depp is so tacky now. As you say, many once-transgressive and stylish people rejected hierarchies of taste and embraced tackiness, outrageousness, and shock value. Is that what Depp is doing? I can't tell. I don't see any resemblance between his former self and his current self. His aesthetic trajectory is incoherent to me.

Margarita: Again, I think one of the biggest problems today for artists especially, is what and who influences us, and also the loss of milieus, traditions, and social attitudes. We are influenced solely by media and promotional culture now, more than actual coteries and meaningful social interactions. One of the reasons Winona Ryder and Johnny Depp had interesting style back then has a lot to do with the stylistic framework of the '90s—the last moment for alternative culture in America. When they wore those clothes, they were open to possibilities. And they obviously had great, raw taste. They were still sort of outsiders in the Hollywood industry—half in, half out. But as soon as you become fully enmeshed in an industry and develop a very specific public image and status within it, which is what always happens with fame, then of course celebrities get schooled on what they should do, how they should act, how they should look. And that's part of the process of fame and the horrible victimization of one's identity that happens with it. You lose what is personal in order to appeal to the everyone. That's what fame is. For me, clothing should be one of the key markers of independence, and famous actors inevitably become dependent on the currency of their images, which can only be under one's control for so long. Over time, Ryder felt that her wealth, success, and style should be signified through wearing and being styled by, what I would call, "post-designers" like Marc Jacobs.

Masha: What's interesting about Depp now is that he still sees himself as some bad-boy bohemian, but of course his so-called outsiderness reeks of being bought, which is maybe why it's so tacky now? There is nouveau riche and there is nouveau style, hence the saying that you can't buy style. This takes us back to the fake and the copy you were talking about earlier. Why do you think we used to believe in the identity of clothes (with avant-garde designers, etc.), and the identity of who was wearing them, but don't now? Is it simply because of the commodification and gentrification of everything?

Margarita: Today, everyone, artists included, aspire to be part of the

Johnny Depp and Winona Ryder, 1991

mainstream. There is no alternative culture anymore. No outside. In the past, being against the mainstream—being critical of it—was what motivated radical artists and thinkers. A good recent example is Alain Badiou's public admission that he wants Brad Pitt to star in his film about Plato rather than some (French) character actor, let's say. Even Badiou wants to be part of Hollywood. It suggests that even Badiou feels that outsiderness has no real power or value anymore. Like everyone, he seems to believe that his ideas can only be validated through conspiring with the culture industry.

Masha: Yeah, we don't have many serious role models left. Everyone wants total visibility and fame. Even when someone is stylish, it doesn't feel individual or personal. I now feel like I don't know why people wear what they wear these days. It's arbitrary.

I'm interested in style as distance, in the aesthetics of distance, which I learned from you, both directly and indirectly. For me, style as opposed to fashion or trend, is really about finding yourself. Another recent example of this culture industry complicity is Jay-Z's six-hour "Picasso Baby" at Pace Gallery, which has him dancing around with Marina Abramovic, among others—the clip went viral. In fact, someone was just watching it on their laptop next to us in this café in Paris, where we're talking now. Art has become completely tied not just to promotional stunts and spectacles, but the desire for celebrity and institutional alliance. But, as you point out, it used to be highly problemaic to have such commercial motives if you were an artist. Of course, Warhol changed all that.

Margarita: Another issue is the fear of being defined as bourgeois, a fear no one in the art or literary world has anymore. In the past, if someone was too well dressed or lived in some lavish apartment, they were considered bourgeois, both aesthetically and intellectually. This bohemian fear, of course, was subverted, as you say, by Warhol who said there is nothing more bourgeois than being afraid of being bourgeois.

Masha: That's funny. This statement is of course very dialectical, both true and untrue. If your Aunt Lydia was your earliest influence, you and cinema were definitely mine. I remember being obsessed with using clothes to fashion certain identities and outsider positions for myself from a very early age. Posing as these characters—usually androgynous, loner boys from movies—like James Dean and Ralph Macchio from *The Outsiders*. I wore what and who I felt I was *inside*. And, of course, my whole sense of style came from inside (i.e., my family, hand-me-downs, movies) as well, from you and dad. So, style was completely linked with my internal life for me, something originary. I always saw clothes as a way of being different, and like you, used them to emphasize—not mask—my difference; to protect it, even when it cost me popularity and social acceptance, which it often did. I never saw clothes as a way in. I saw them as a way out, and you always encouraged that. I can't remember you ever telling me not to wear something and sometimes what I wore to school was pretty weird (different colored socks; mismatched earrings that I made myself; ripped tights; different sneakers on each foot; crazy haircuts). My fondest memory of your style influences on me was dreaming about going to the Oscars in one of your outfits to accept an award for best actress. It never occurred to me that I would have my own clothes as an adult and that time would inevitably change what I would wear! I wanted to wear your wild outfits like Cher in her Oscar dresses in the '80s. I loved her then. No one dresses like that now, and if they do, it's a promotional stunt dreamed up by a chain of stylists and PR people—like Lady Gaga. The difference is: I believe Cher's outfit; I don't believe Gaga's.

So there are a few photographs I wanted to look at with you now that document how your style evolved over the years. Can you take me through some of these pictures?

Margarita: Sure.

PART II:

Margarita Tupitsyn at the opening of the exhibition "Sots Art: Russian Mock-Heroic Style," which she curated, at Semaphore Gallery, New York City, 1984

Masha: Tell me about this "all red" photo? Where was it taken, what year, and what are you wearing?

Margarita: This is me at the opening of the Sots Art show, which I curated in 1984 for Semaphore Gallery in Soho. In the background is a fragment of the painting by the Russian artist Aleksandr Kosolapov. In this photo I am still taking advantage of my aunt Lydia's designs. She made this outfit. I'm still in my pre-Japanese designers phase. Lydia is applying Kazimir Malevich's Suprematist, geometric forms to clothing. She would also make accessories for the clothes. As you can see, I am wearing her earrings in the photograph. So the idea of "total" design is being taken from the Russian avant-garde—the idea that everything, when it comes to style and design, has to coalesce. You can also see that my hair is already shorter, and cut asymmetrically, echoing the clothes and the earrings. It is not cut off completely yet, but it is no longer the classically long hair I'd always had before that. When I was at the CUNY graduate center, studying for my PhD in Art History with Rosalind Krauss and other important art historians, my classmates would always comment on my long hair and how it made me look like a pre-Raphaelite. So, to reject this, I started cutting my hair shorter and shorter.

Masha Tupitsyn and Margarita Tupitsyn
at the opening of the exhibition "Iskunstvo: Berlin-Moscow," Moscow, 1989

Masha: You were already subverting classical notions of female beauty to spite your beauty. I love this next photo, where we're looking at each other. This is in Moscow, during Perestroika. We are at the opening of Iskunstvo, an art exhibition of German and Russian artists. The title, as you explained to me, is a play between the German and Russian word for art. You and dad had moved to Moscow for a year to work on the Russian edition of the Italian art magazine *Flash Art*, and you were also publishing your first book, *Margins of Soviet Art: Socialist Realism to the Present*. We had just come from Milan, where we lived for six months, and where I became interested in clothes in a way that was also feminine, not just masculine or androgynous. I stopped being a tomboy in Milan. I grew out my hair and became obsessed with knee-highs and tights, which is an obsession that continues to this day, one that you and I both share. In this photo, you're wearing a fabulous nautical-inspired Jean Paul Gaultier dress, which I now have. You're also wearing the Italian designer Emilio Cavallini. This is an interesting photo because it shows another side of your aesthetic. All your hair is cut off now, but you are not just wearing austere Japanese designers. You also wore "sexier" designers like Gaultier and Dolce & Gabbana and Romeo Gigli, a great '90s Italian designer, who played with ideas of sexiness. But with Gaultier, and especially in your case, you deconstructed and subverted femininity and sexiness by pairing it up with the more austere and cerebral contemporary Japanese clothing you wore. You never played it straight, as it were. You always made sure to combine different aesthetics. For example, you would wear that amazing red satin Gaultier bra top, with the pointed breasts, which you did *before* Madonna, by the way, but with some austere clownish black CDG kulats. Also, look at the knee-highs you're wearing in this picture—the garters are on the knee instead of the thigh, which I find really smart and funny.

Margarita: Yeah, those knee-highs were amazing. But I am also wearing these big '60s-inspired glasses, like the ones you wear now, and that '60s pillbox style bag, so there are all kinds of styles at play. I don't know why I didn't keep those gorgeous Cavallini shoes. What happened to them? But anyway, that's what was interesting about all these different influences. It was an interesting period for Italian design, too.

Masha: Right, the kind of dresses you see Sophia Loren wearing in neo-realist Italian films, which of course wasn't cheesy at the time but quite elegant. Or Brigitte Bardot. It had elegance despite being a hyper-feminine exalting of the female form. You see this in Fellini films, too, though Fellini always had a kind of early Gaultier approach to beauty ideals—he always made everything beautiful grotesque or strange, like with Masina in *La Strada*, as you mentioned earlier. He deformed beauty. One of the problems is that famous design labels have been taken over by a new generation of designers, with entirely different backgrounds and aesthetics, so the aesthetics of Chanel and Gucci, etc., totally shifted, the original context severed. These fashion houses were not yet these super corporate conglomerations of mass-produced, mass-circulated brand designs.

Margarita: And the new incarnation of designers have only ever worked in that kind of corporate structure, so they are jaded from the start, and don't even fully cultivate or oversee their own designs. They treat it as a business and corporate brand first and foremost, and a creative endeavor second. The aesthetic is fractured into a lot of unseen forces—input—but only one person takes sole credit. And because *couture*, or at least the circulation of it, is now mass-produced and infinitely copied, the people who design it don't have a sense of the value of originality and quality. Moreover, because they don't have any real creative control over it, they no longer feel obliged to design well. Trends intensify and accelerate and quality degrades. It benefits the design industry as a whole. They know all their designs will be copied by chains anyway. The gap between original and mass-produced, between quantity and quality, is getting smaller and smaller. Nothing is made well anymore, and if it is, it costs a fortune and only the richest people have access to it. But it is also important to point out that different things look different on different people. It's not just total style, it's total effect—context. We're constantly being told what looks good and what people should wear. What I used to like about shopping at Japanese stores like CDG is that they were empty. But more importantly, I was left alone. They didn't try to sell you things. Nor did they pamper you with lies about how you looked in something when you tried it on.

Masha: You had to form your own opinion about what you were buying and wearing. Form your own personal connection to style.

Margarita: Yeah, the shop assistants wouldn't say anything. If someone tells you that you look good in something, but you don't *feel* it, it doesn't really matter what the thing itself looks like or how great it is. It's a sales pitch. I remember in the '90s already, when you would come to the Yohji Yamamoto store in Soho, the shop assistants started doing that. Being bothered, or aggressively "sold" something went against my approach to style. I wanted to experience clothes like a work of art—thinking about it, contemplating it. I wanted to decide if I liked something myself. Contemporary Japanese designers were the same way; they were sort of copying this ascetic, gallery-distant attitude. It was bad taste in galleries at that time to jump on viewers who came to look at the work. It's propaganda, which is what fashion—and art—has been reduced to. If you tell people that everyone will look good in the same things, it's propaganda. It's conformity. It's advertising.

Masha: It reminds me of that famous Pygmalion scene in *Pretty Woman* (1990)—a little nod to Preston Sturges' *The Palm Beach Story*, I suspect—when Richard Gere gives Julia Roberts his credit card to buy an entire new wardrobe on Rodeo Drive. She's completely redecorated like a doll by the shop assistants who had previously refused to sell her anything because of the way she looked. All the aesthetic choices are made on her behalf, which is treated as a celebratory, triumphant moment in the film. Vivian has finally passed for a "real" lady. But I preferred the way she looked before! At least those "sex worker" clothes were *her* choices. Her reality. Being dressed up—impersonally styled by everyone at the store—is perceived as the highest mark of flattery and economic privilege—an indoctrination into polite bourgeois society and traditional femininity.

Margarita: But that's a very important issue that we discussed yesterday. The fact that everyone gets dressed up by "tastemakers" now. The minute people have money, they stop dressing themselves. There is a loss of autonomy and agency that happens with fame. These tastemakers are only concerned with making money and bringing money to the

Left: Margarita Tupitsyn in the studio of Vladimir Nemukhin, Moscow, 1987

designers they promote. It's about affiliations and promotion rather than attitudes and preferences.

Masha: In an interview about his early anti-fashion Culture Club looks, Boy George stated, "Most fashion is about wearing money." Which brings us to the idea of the mainstreaming of the avant-garde and the mainstreaming of style, which while good in theory, as you point out, in consumer capitalism has killed individual style and aesthetic agency. There is a whole industry behind teaching people what to wear now and "making people over." The modernist idea in the '40s and '50s, by all-around designers like Eames, was that you could mass-produce quality. It was believed that everyone should be able to own beautiful things for not a lot of money. Now it's the mass production of cheapness, which is, in fact, not a democratization at all. Most people have shit and only a few people have quality. It's actually a widening of the gap between those who can have well-made, durable things and those who can't. What is built to last and what is built to fall apart. And getting things cheap always means there is an increasingly long global chain of exploitation.

Margarita: Bauhaus envisioned this affordable model of quality before Eames. Take Mies van der Rohe's furniture, which is now very expensive but was originally meant to be affordable. And yet, his furniture was always the property of rich people, so that ideal only functioned in theory in this case. But as I was saying yesterday, the Russian avant-garde and Bauhaus had this utopia of good taste, of quality mass-production, but this utopian vision has obviously failed. It ended up being generic and shoddy, like IKEA. Nothing at IKEA is built to last in any sense. In fact, it's disposability that has come to stand for quality and style.

Masha: And what about this final picture?

Margarita Tupitsyn at the opening of the exhibition
"The Work of Art in the Age of Perestroika," which she curated, at
the Phyllis Kind Gallery, New York City, 1990

Margarita: This is me at Phyllis Kind gallery in Soho, where I curated my exhibition, "The Work of Art in the Age of Perestroika" in 1990. The painting I'm standing next to is by the artist Vadim Zakharov and Viktor Skersis. Here you can see that my style has once again completely changed. I look like a little boy! My hair is cut off, and I was only wearing Japanese designers at that point. This is the black CDG raincoat that you wear now, by the way. It's a men's coat. But again, I am wearing a Constructivist-style red Russian watch and a big blue ring that Lydia made. But what's interesting is, at that time, in 1990, it wasn't just about looking good or cool, or having some hip style, like it is in the art world today. It was more about wearing things that reflected a personal attitude—a little bit severe, conceptual, intellectual, critical—grouchy! So these clothes conveyed that internal stance. It was important for me and other artists and intellectuals at that time to wear clothes that reflected how we felt and thought. These clothes were my identity. The identity of the art world in the '80s and '90s was probably the last time when this was true.

Masha: I wear that trench coat now. Every few years I have to fix it with a tailor. It is one of my favorite pieces of clothing. For me, the '90s were really important because I was lucky enough to be a teenager in a still relatively culturally dynamic and nonconformist time. There was still some possibility of an alternative culture, so my sense of identity, femininity, and style wasn't being completely mediated or prescribed by corporate consumer culture. Being independent was still really important to me and everyone I knew. Today even much of the subculture comes from some highly visible and branded place. Granted, I know a lot of my sense of personal autonomy and freedom as an adolescent came from being a New Yorker, having you and dad as parents, going to LaGuardia, a public art high school, where being different was actually encouraged, so I never felt any pressure to be anyone other than myself. Everyone hung out with everyone—a very rare high school experience, I know. Obviously, that played a big part in my personal and creative development. Nevertheless, I do see it as a profoundly different time.

TIMEPIECE (THE NEW ROMANTICS)

"Music is the perfect place to live."[103]
—Dave Gahan, 2017

Music? Is that you? Where have you been? I've truly missed you.

Now we return to the golden age of music.

33 years....such a magnificent sound! Anybody listening in 2020?

Since 1998 not a single day without it.

2021 and I'm still listening to it!

2020 and hard to say it's the last century.

Im listening to it here in year 5300. Time travellers like me love songs from the past.

Never grows old. We plan to time travel again in the 80s! My favorite era! Cheers!!

[103]. In the 1945 film adaptation of *The Picture of Gray*, Dorian asks his love interest, the singer and actress Sibyl Vane, "What does music mean to you?" She replies: "I don't know. It's full of emotion, but it's not happy." In Jean-Jacques Beineix's *Diva*, 1981, a celebrated 33 year old American opera singer, who refuses to record her performances, is told: "A voice isn't eternal."

Sound of the future!!!

Bring us "Going Backwards"!

My God this seems like yesterday. Getting old is weird.

Good music is never old.

One of the best songs. And the year im born.

Wow they were so young.

How young we were!

Wonder what the people at the concert remember about this performance.

I was ten years old...

Still listen in my 50tys....)).

I was born in that year.

he was a baby then.

Within 1 second of watching this video and listening to their music, my youth has come back.

1998 - STRANGELOVE !!!
2019 - STRANGELOVE !!!
3090 - STRANGELOVE !!!

Oh God, take me back to this time. I miss it!

I'm 28 and...not sure what that has to do with anything.

decades girl, 73, 83, 93. Decades.

I'm about to be born and I'm so in love with this band.

I was born in the wrong generation.

I know, he is so fine. I'm 24 ;).

I'm little 15 but I love depeche Mode!

Teenage Mode.

Not teenage, but surely twentyage.

My God, they look like babies here!

Love them, and I'm 25. Dave Gahan was so handsome and still is.

I'm 14 and love this song.

Im 9 and i love this song.

Im 41 years old...

Funny how time flies...

2021?

January 22nd 2021.....6.45pm....I am on the clock here in 60160 zipcode Melrose Park Illinois listening to this beautiful song from the 80's....Thank you for posting this....much appreciated.

whos listening in 1988!!!!! There will be a pandemic in 2020? I dont even know what that means. It is 1988.

Oh the yearning for the 80s is very strong tonight. If, like me, you lived your youth through the 80s (I was born in 1970), I salute you.

I wish I could go back to these days when life was so simple and great!!!!!!!!!! Lets go back............ ...whos coming with me?????

This was my favorite song growing up.

Like. The most romantic love song ever written. Ever.

She came back into my life briefly after 7 years apart, I messed things up when I had her. I looked for this song everywhere and couldn't find it for the life of me. She was driving and focusing on the road and I couldn't help but just stare at her. She slipped through my fingers and here I am.

I like this Song all the Time.

0:04
4:26
4:39

What great memories.

here after hearing the 2020 election results.

This is what I call a time machine song.

If only I had been born at least 10 years earlier. 😔

Help Im stuck in a tangent universe.

Have you ever seen a portal?

Its weird that on Xmas Eve I fell into this rabbit hole. This was one of my favorite albums as a teenager. I'm 51.

Everyone wishes they could relive the 80s... you can...get out there and live, dammit... that's all we did then... just lived.

I'm lost in admiration, could I need you this much? Oh, you're wasting my time You're just just just wasting time 💔

I used to listen to this driving around in my HQ Holden back in 1987. This was the first DM song I ever heard in early 1984 when I was 10 years old. Never forget that moment. I bought Construction Time Again and then it wasn't long until People are People, Master and Servant and Some Great Reward were released. Been a fan since then and I've seen DM 3 times (86, 90 and 01).

The memories this song evokes in me are so vivid and I long to go back to when this album came out. I was in Rome with great friends, some no longer with us. We were so young and untouchable then. We listened to such incredible music back then. rock, electro pop, indie, goth, Nick Cave and Joy Division, Bowie and Sabbath. Great times.

the olympic games in los angeles in 1984...that was the times of the so-called cold war...it made me think of my schooldays...briliant music and lyrics...one of the top songs of the 20th Century...

Purple Rain soundtrack was the first album I ever bought when I was a kid. I have been a Prince fan since I was a little girl and I still LOVE him. Prince will forever be the Greatest of all Time.

1988 ENJOYING IN DOWNEY CALIFORNIA 2021 ENJOYING IN DOWNEY CALIFORNIA. STILL ROCKING.

Remember high school.

The best years of my life....I remember being at a party around 1989... somebody played the big LP....I was fascinated....I remember that party...that exact time...as if it happened last weekend.

the first time I heard this was when it opened the Black Celebration tour in 1986, Los Angeles Forum -- all the lights went out and they played this in total darkness, it was then followed by the song Black

Celebration - an experience I will never forget.

That's when l first heard it also. 1986 Bristol Hippodrome.

It segued right into the song Black Celebration. I saw them at Southern Star Amphitheater in Houston, 1986.

I will always remember the moment, when they played this song during a concert back in the early 90s in Zurich. A friend of mine and me were about 5 meters away from the stage. We had seen the movie before and memorized the lyrics, so we started to sing along at the top of our lungs. Nobody else around us knew this song yet. That's when Martin made eye contact with me and smiled.

This song has always stayed with me.

This song makes me so emotional.

i want to cry when i listen to this song...

crying.

a list of weirdly specific things this song reminds me of:
-being 7 years old at goodwill and my mom is telling me not to sit on the floral couch that (probably) belonged to a woman who died of lung cancer at age 70 from smoking two packs a day (this is a good memory)
-in that same vein, ugly still lifes at goodwill that (probably) belonged to the same person as the couch previously mentioned. both the couch and the paintings are painfully out of style and matronly, but in my seven year old mind theyre beautiful and timeless and transport me to worlds of fairies and witches and mermaids and such. they still do. i say "ugly" and "matronly" in the sence that youd only really find them in the thrift store because they remind people of old ladies who died of lung cancer at age 70 from smoking two packs a day. im getting off topic –
-shittily edited and poorly dubbed 4kidz anime (specifically the tokyo

mew mew dub) that sparked my imagination as a kid to start writing stories and creating my own characters
-bringing my nintendo DS everywhere as a kid
-in the car driving over bridges and looking out at the water on a sunny day
-tall buildings.
each chord strike like a pyle driven column forming the foundation of a perfectly designed architectural monolith.

I wish I was there.

1988—this song is amazing! 2020—this song is amazing!

I just heard it on the radio...first time... It is perfect, amazing... I have no words.

Send this off to the Cosmos!

Forever.

Who's listening to this matchless piece in Year 2020 in Corona Pandemic times?

Who is listening to this song in 2020?

Who's listening to this in 2025?

I'm watching from 2029.

A shameless and hack question, but "hear" goes anyway: 'Who's listening in 2021!?

I love this song ...december 2020 total quarantine from Chile. 🖐

20 years old and this is still a fresh, dark, catchy and unique sound!

38 years ago today.

Me, in 2020.

One of the best songs ever written. Brings back so many memories, especially my fifteenth birthday.

Beautiful song. 80s music will live forever.

God, I miss the 90s.

His voice is so smooth and powerful at the same time…Sometimes I forget how much time has passed. Seems like yesterday. 🌷🖤

This sound is why I'd rather be stuck in the past. Makes me relive my youth more clearly and it is much more fun. 🖤

This song is straight up Hypnosis.

It builds and builds.

Goosebumps.

Always with me! Again and again....

Awesome way to get to tears—returning to my past life.

my life story.

reminds me of when i was younger.

I was born with this song.

1988 - this song is amazing!
2020 - this song is amazing!
2030 - this song is amazing!
2040 - this song is amazing!
2050 - this song is amazing!
2060 - this song is amazing!
2070 - this song is amazing!

32 years and it is still a pleasure to listen to this...

1985???

No. Video is 1987!

This is 86-88. Prince did not use horns in 1984.

The song isn't from 84!

1984??? Come on NOW!!!

What year is this?

It's not 1983.

So like 40.

1988 and almost the end of the world. I'm blessed.

Extended versions of songs are always so much better.

and many of them are "hidden."

what about the old fadeout in songs? they don't to do that much these days.

A fadeout in a song means: etc etc etc.

in movies, it's called exit music.

It means it carries on.

now songs just END.

yea, going nowhere!

Its like we're being ghosted by a song.

i would always play the songs in order on albums and chase the fades.

i'd turn up the volume to catch every last drop of the Record because some of the best stuff was in the fade.

Remember secret tracks?

Secret tracks were for the die-hard fans.

Hidden tracks are a peek into an alternate universe, clues into the world of an album.

A magic box.

I remember my first encounter with an interlude, back in 2001, with System of a Down's Toxicity. I'd heard that if you punch in the number 15 in the CD player you would hear the hidden track. I couldn't believe when it worked.

interludes are transitions between songs. they're for catching your breath.

movies and albums used to have interludes.

they can appear anywhere—beginning middle end.

but you gotta listen the whole way through…!

I've never heard this one before. Where did you find it?

Its a bonus track. There are 3 different versions floating around somewhere.

None of them are on the studio album.

anyone have links?

Listen to their soundchecks. 83-90.

Intros, outros.

It's only 1 minute.

It's the continuation of enjoy the silence.

the melody is from Strangelove

Even shorter. 53 seconds.

not even a minute-long, and its a masterpiece.

this is epic.

Love this little Gem. Like the ending of Pimpf.

Feel its a bit pre-emptive of Dream On.

The hidden interlude of Blue Dress is 30 sec.

Anyone know what the song at 1:42 mins is??

Laurent Petitgand—Excitement. I know I'm repsonding 6 yrs later, but better late than never.

Death's Door.

their track for Until the End of the World.

I'm looking for all the 'b' sides that I lost back when my cassettes & remixes were stolen!

thank you for putting all these interludes here.

oh man..I had these gems on tape back in the 80's and 90's...Lost them unfortunately...So good to hear them again.

Die-hards are going to go insane for this.

Let them ALL out!

So difficult to get behind-the-scenes, rehearsal action especially from the Wilder-era. Love how they mucked around with 'Somebody'. I'm totally blown away by these audio takes. Thank you.

00:02 Schüttorf 28.5.1983 - My secret garden (instrumental)
04:23 Mannheim 10.12.1983 - Everything counts (instrumental/full band)
11:56 Ludwigshafen 21.11.1984 - Something to do (instrumental, take 1)
15:59 Ludwigshafen 21.11.1984 - Something to do (instrumental, take 2)
18:51 Munich, 1.12.1984 - Something to do (full band, take 1)
23:22 Munich, 1.12.1984 - Something to do (full band, take 2)
27:47 Munich, 1.12.1984 - Somebody (Martin & Alan)
30:06 Stockholm 26.4.1986 - Black celebration (full band)
36:28 Stockholm 26.4.1986 - It doesn't matter two (full band)
39:26 London 12.2.1988 - Just can't get enough (full band)
45:41 London 12.2.1988 - Behind the wheel (instrumental)
56:09 Stockholm 12.2.1988 - Behind the wheel (instrumental, take 1)
58:43 Stockholm 12.2.1988 - Strangelove (full band)
1:01:47 Stockholm 12.2.1988 - Behind the wheel (full band, take 2)
1:07:40 Stockholm 12.2.1988 - Pipeline (full band)
1:12:28 Gothenburg 5.10.1990 - World in my eyes (full band, take 1)
1:18:07 Gothenburg 5.10.1990 - World in my eyes (full band, take 2)

Can´t explain how much I love at 3:08.

3:05-3:22, that part is so damn good.

Loop forever.

Such a massive, monumental, beautiful sound. This is how its done, kids. Just imagine the era that produced this. Man, we had it good.

We really did.

You guys are lucky af.

90's TEENS!!!!!

Post-punk, pre-dance/techno. This was the zenith.

He lives in this song. This lives in my heart.

He is soo young here ...

And soooo beautiful.

Just watch Meaning of Love. Now that is young. That is beautiful.

I miss his young voice.

It's changed. But all singing voices change as we age. He's at his peak here.

im too late to fall in love with a boy who is 52 years old now.

i can't remember how many times I've bought Purple Rain over the years on cassette tape and on CD.

Same. Vinyl, cassette, CD, Spotify.

A song that outlives us all.

A genius lives forever.

His music is timeless. I listen every day.

Classics never die.

Did somebody say I miss the 80s?!

Energy on the dance floor in the 80s was unbelievable. If you didn't leave the floor soaking wet...you did it all wrong.

Millennials got only 8GB memory for their entire life. These are poor people who are unable to enjoy the moment.

Ain't that the Truth?!?

Pathetic it is.

They are playing one of DM's biggest hits literally ten feet away from you and you're on your phone filming. So sad.

Right!? Man.

Yeah, kids are ridiculous these days. It's almost like they forgot how to just enjoy something without filming it to post on social media to get likes.

They're not even there, they're just there for the posts.

Yeah, the 80s where you can see the Band onstage instead of all the SMARTPHONES.

There was something unique about the 80s that will never be replicated. I cannot put my finger on it.

80's had more HEART (and soul).

Back then, music truly was tracking the pulse of our soul, so every hit that came out was actually yanked out of our soul. It was us screaming. Every note was actually the very fibre of ourselves. That's why we felt liberated. As opposed to music now. We feel trapped. I hope I'm making sense.

When the artists were originals and free spirited, not fake and programmed.

Once in a lifetime artists.

Her voice was so strong. You can feel every word. Just straight-up-music. Quality regardless of genre. No Auto-Tune, no back up music, just Tina and the band. Hard to find real music like this nowadays.

She was Killer live.

I was there!

Being at this concert was electrifying.

I wish i could build a time machine and attend this concert.

Listen all you young singers of today, this is the real thing. No tricks, no B.S. All gut, true blues. Today this music sounds like counter-culture.

The music in today's charts is poor. Pop music is dead, ruined, and buried by the casting shows and their puppets.

"Let me hear you make decisions without your television." They were always ahead of their time.

Let me hear you make decisions without your smartphone.

Ancient video buried for centuries came up in 2020...

Gonna take my tiimmme ... I have all the time in the woooorld.

Everytimeeverywhere.

25. October. 2020. Forever DM!!!

This song is still the best. Omg 36 years <3.

O.M.G. I remember listening to this on cassette in my bedroom when I was in High School.

Remember cranking this LOUD in my Nissan Maxima ... through Los Angeles nights, 1997-98.

I remember hearing it as a teenager and thinking, "they understand."

Ah to be 15 again and listening to this for the first time.

To be 17.

To be 26.

To be there.

wish I could go back to the 90s.

I used this song in 88 as a song book report. Landed me in the counselor's office. I'm still alive. Lol.

I'm 42 and I think from as far as I can remember never heard better lyrics. I dedicate that song to my possible future girlfriend/wife if I ever have one. Will return here if that happens. Wish me luck.

Didn't realize this is an 8-year-old thread.

I am hanging by a single thread.

This song keeps me alive.

i woke up with these lyrics in my mind.

This made me nostalgic even though I was born in 94'

Celebrating 30 years of VIOLATOR here! Who's with me!

30 years already? I was in my early twenties. Still loving this, more than ever!

May 2020 - lockdown blues. A classic. Timeless.

79 to 99. Best part of our society. Best years of their music.

After 2K in calendar its worse and worse day by day.

2029 anyone?

It's been three years. We all miss 2017, a simple time. The world is in flames and Covid is killing everyone.

"Ordinary acts of fun have been diluted.
Place it in your memory
Leave it in your past
But don't forget."

This is my end of the world song of the night.

This song could be included in the soundtrack of Terminator 2 - Judgement Day.

The last two minutes are the end of the world.¹⁰⁴

104. "Timepiece" is an assemblage of YouTube comments on a number of 1980s and 1990s bands I listened to during 2020. I constructed this piece by combing through thousands of YouTube comments that in some cases span years, but crescendoed and congregated around the subject of pandemic-time in 2020-2021. I have spliced these comments with my own writing. The philosopher Jean-Luc Nancy writes in *L'Intrus* (his personal account—"is it a speech or a novel? I don't know," asks Claire Denis, who adapted Nancy's unadaptable text into a film in 2004) of his miraculous heart transplant, "Here personal contingency crosses with contingency in the history of technology." I believe this also applies to music in the COVID streaming era.

AFTERWORD

Masha Tupitsyn's *Time Tells* begins with an elegiac reflection on time that demonstrates the profoundly moving possibilities of the poetic essay. Recalling Roland Barthes' *Camera Lucida* and Susan Sontag's *Styles of Radical Will*, Tupitsyn's writing merges memoir, novel, and philosophy in a mode of critique that cannot be reduced to a particular object or subject, but is rather a way of being. In *Time*, she constructs her own rhapsodic and ecstatic *kairos*, which, as she explains, is a sensuous counterpoint to the merely chronological *kronos*, and amalgamates insights through an expansive lattice of temporal analogies. As with her previous work in other forms—from *Love Dog* and *LACONIA* to her durational films *Love Sounds* and *DECADES*—a diverse array of material is held together in *Time* by an intensely focused compositional drive. The phenomenologies and circadian rhythms of lived time at the center of Tupitsyn's book are not simply documented using a chronology of data accumulation. Instead, she recomposes contemporary life in all its dense complexity with inventiveness and penetrating acumen. There is a reverence for music in *Time* that is itself musically articulated. The pensive cadences of Tupitsyn's writing crescendo to passionate denouements in a recurring fugue structure (not coincidentally, Tupitsyn was trained as a classical pianist). As she observes, music is what we look to in the aftermath of time, and her own writing is composed of movements that elude normative progressions.

Tupitsyn's musical phenomenology is also an epistemology of genre. How, she asks, does timing alternately compose (and decompose) the musical, the cinematic, the comedy standup, acting, the social media feed? How does timing (*kairos*) itself disappear into what she calls digital homeostasis? Tupitsyn does not answer these questions from an Archimedean point of presentist omnipotence in the manner of a dogmatic media theorist. She shows what it is like to actually live in and feel through our current world without submitting to the digital vortex of postmodern cynicism. Her book carefully charts how one can extract oneself from the digital marketplace of time and content-production without retreating into a utopian fantasy or intellectual void. She weaves connections between genres, films, politics, books, media platforms, and styles without rushing to easy or gratifying conclusions. As Tupitsyn recollects and remembers pieces of our cultural past, she ingeniously elucidates the elusive present in a form capacious enough to interlace YouTube comments, a searing analysis on the role of time in David Fincher's *Zodiac*, and a candid interview about the transgressive philosophy of style with her mother, the art historian Margarita Tupitsyn. In this way, she follows in the constellatory footsteps of Walter Benjamin. Dwelling with mementos of the past, Tupitsyn's digital arcades—with their green flashes of technical brilliance—become a pathway towards a renewed desire for life as well as new ways of potentially making time.[1]

The reinvention of time cannot be rushed. Only by enduring the coming and going of time itself can time have the chance to matter again. We need to move past the double-bind of an addictogenic culture that forces us to choose between eternal emptiness and eternal fullness. The search for lost time may seem futile at this point—unlike in Proust, it is now time itself, not moments of time, that is lost. And yet, like in Proust, for Tupitsyn the futility of recovery opens up the intrinsic pleasures and possibilities of searching (the narrator of *À la recherche du temps perdu* confesses to a bad memory: the delight in recollection

---

1. As Miriam Hansen puts it, the elaboration of Benjamin's work comes not from merely clarifying his ideas but also resuming, in the present, his "concern for the conditions of apperception, sensorial affect, and cognition, experience and memory," forming what she calls "a political ecology of the senses." (Miriam Hansen, "Why Media Aesthetics," *Critical Inquiry*, Vol. 30, No. 2, 2004–5).

is premised by an impossible task). Tupitsyn knows that it is precisely through comprehending the enormity and gravity of cultural loss and materiality that one can cherish the remains—no matter how profane; like the shattered fragments that hold together the potential for divine spark in Benjamin. In retrospective light (the light of cinema being another imaginative leitmotif that runs through *Time*), the anachronistic, as Tupitsyn illustrates, can disclose previously unthinkable political possibilities. The illuminations that run through the book find the sacred in the discounted and offers an alternative to popular film criticism that overrates classics and celebrates cliches. In "Interlude," for example, she invites us to recall the magic of *Pretty Woman* and, in doing so, not only explains its particular—less obvious—appeal, but shows us new ways of being enchanted. Unlike the monetized nostalgia of the major streaming services, Tupitsyn refuses to affirm the past as an unblemished ideal, instead prioritizing and politicizing the mediation and temporalization of *reception*.

For Tupitsyn, the stains of time and technology cannot be wiped away. In *Time*, the roughness of the glitch, the painstakingness of mediation, is shown to be always already part of the *miracle* of aesthetic form. The total plenum of unconcealed presence is precisely the loss of loss this book zealously works against. Tupitsyn pursues a dialectic of concealment and revelation that shows us new ways to think about and make art. Her memories are refracted through the stains of the archive. "Green scenes" return throughout the book as ways to allow the *punctum* to pierce through the coded 24/7 digital apparatus—whether by discussing the literal green flash in *Call Me by Your Name* or the way an unexpected '80s or '90s music video on YouTube in 2020 can trigger the analog memory of a forgotten paradigm, like Proust's Madeleine. As Tupitsyn puts it about the 20th century reign of cinema: "The thing you lost or never found is no longer simply a person or a movie but a time in which it was possible to entertain the premise that you could want to live your wish, the wish of life itself. That you would be here to receive it." These flashes of memory—and faith—pierce the didactic limitations of theory, which often go no further than pitting technology against poetics or unifying them. In *Time*, the digital is shown to have reified and coded time, desire, and memory to such an extent that everything is exposed and nothing is mysterious enough anymore to invite contemplation or pause. The way out is not by obliterating the machines or offering the artificial supplement promised by mindfulness apps. Time, Tupitsyn argues, must be ongoingly sought after and actively reconstituted. Lived. It cannot simply be made to exist somewhere outside of technology or in the trappings of nostalgia. Tupitsyn creates gaps, intermissions, and delays in the ruthless "flow" of information; powerfully resurrecting time, even as it incessantly passes away.

—Felix Bernstein, New York City, 2021

APPENDIX

Images by order of appearance:

1. *The X-Files*, 1993
2. *The Sopranos*, 1999
3. *Matchstick Men*, 2003
4. "I Can't Fucking Breathe," NYC, 2020, photo by Masha Tupitsyn
5. *Varda by Agnes*, 2018
6. *Until the End of the World*, 1991-1994
7. *Home of the Brave*, 1986
8. *Home for the Holidays*, 1995
9. Love is Telepathic, NYC, 2015, photo by Masha Tupitsyn
10. *The Green Ray*, 1986
11. *Bell, Book, and Candle*, 1958
12. *Northern Exposure*, 1991
13. *The Kominsky Method*, 2018
14. *Sebastian Maniscalco: Why Would You Do That?*, 2016
15. *You*, 2018
16. *Easy*, 2016
17. *Frances Ha*, 2013
18. *Call Me by Your Name*, 2017
19. *Pretend It's a City*, 2021
20. *Notebook on Cities and Clothes*, 1989
21. *That Damn Michael Che*, 2021
22. *Cleo from 5 to 7*, 1962
23. *Sun Don't Shine*, 2012
24. *The Net*, 1995
25. *I Used to Go Here*, 2020
26. *Gertrud*, 1964
27. *Broadcast News*, 1987
28. *Frances Ha*, 2013
29. *In the Soup*, 1992
30. *Locations: Looking for Rusty James,* on *Rumble Fish*, 2013

31. *Doctor Zhivago*, 1965
32. *Jeremiah Johnson*, 1972
33. *Barry Lyndon*, 1975
34. *2001: A Space Odyssey*, 1968
35. *Lightning Over Water*, 1980
36. *L'intrus*, 2004
37. *Drive*, 2011
38. *Varda by Agnes*, 2018
39. *The Hit*, 1984
40. *Manhunter*, 1986
41. *Serendipity*, 2001
42. *The Cobweb*, 1955
43. *Broadcast News*, 1987
44. *That Touch of Mink*, 1962
45. *Sex Lies and Videotape*, 1989
46. *A.I. Artificial Intelligence*, 2001
47. *A Faithful Man*, 2019
48. *Tenet*, 2021
49. *Varda by Agnes*, 2019
50. *Young Ahmed*, 2019
51. *Red Notice*, 2021
52. *Gorillas in the Mist*, 1988
53. *One Sings, The Other Doesn't*, 1976
54. *Possessed*, 1931
55. Yasujiru Ozu's stop watch, *Tokyo-ga*, 1985
56. *Indiscreet*, 1958
57. *Highlander*, 1985
58. *The Way We Were*, 1973
59. *2046*, 2004
60. *Behind the Scenes: 2046*, 2004
61. *Zodiac*, 2007
62. *Basic Instinct*, 1992
63. *Dead Pool*, 1998
64. *Zodiac*, 2007
65. *The Exorcist III*, 1990
66. *Zodiac*, 2007

67. *Thief*, 1982
68. *Zodiac*, 2007
69. *Manhunter*, 1986
70. *Day of the Dead*, 1985
71. *Donnie Darko*, 2001
72. *Zodiac*, 2007
73. *The Unseen*, 1996
74. *Zodiac*, 2007
75. *The Enforcer*, 1976
76. *Widows*, 2018
77. *Zodiac*, 2007
78. *The Sopranos*, 1999
79. *One Sings, The Other Doesn't*, 1976
80. *We Are Who We Are*, 2020
81. *Berliner Ballade*, 1990
82. *Katt Williams: World War III*, 2022
83. *Kevin Hart: Zero F**ks Given*, 2020
84. *Demolition Man*, 1993
85. *Northern Exposure*, 1990
86. *Violets are Blue*, 1986
87. Adam Horowitz, Press interview, 1992
88. *We Are Who We Are*, 2020
89. *Let Them All Talk*, 2020
90. *Audrey*, 2020
91. *Tenet*, 2021
92. *Cleo from 5 to 7*, 1962
93. Richard Grannon, YouTube, 2021
94. *Seinfeld*, 1996

Previous Publications:

Earlier versions of "Time Machine" and "The Year of Magical Thinking" first appeared in *The Los Angeles Review of Books Quarterly Journal: The Pop issue*, No. 26, in Spring 2020.

An earlier version of "Green Scene" first appeared in *Your Impossible Voice*, Issue Twenty-Three, Fall 2020.

"2014 (The Age of Style)" first appeared in *Berfois* as "The Art of Style: An Interview between Margarita Tupitsyn and Masha Tupitsyn" on June 9, 2014 and was excerpted in *Women in Clothes*, Penguin, 2014.

The final version of "2014 (The Age of Style)," appeared in *Interlude Docs*, document 077, ed. Rebekah Weikel, Aug.19 2022, https://interludedocs.com/2022/08/doc-077-masha-tupitsyn/.

ABOUT THE AUTHOR

MASHA TUPITSYN is a writer, critic, and multi-media artist. She is the author of *Picture Cycle* (Semiotexte/MIT, 2019), *Like Someone In Love: An Addendum to Love Dog* (Penny-Ante Editions, 2013), *Love Dog* (Penny-Ante Editions, 2013), *LACONIA: 1,200 Tweets on Film* (ZerO Books, 2011), *Beauty Talk & Monsters*, a collection of film-based stories (Semiotext(e) Press, 2007), and co-editor of the anthology *Life As We Show It: Writing on Film* (City Lights, 2009).

In 2015, she made the 24-hour film, *Love Sounds*, an audio-essay and history of love in English-speaking cinema, which concluded an immaterial trilogy. The film was accompanied by a catalogue, published in 2015 by Penny-Ante Editions, and has been exhibited and screened in the United States, Canada, Europe, and Australia.

In 2017, she started her ongoing durational film series, *DECADES*. So far, she has completed the 1970s and the 1980s. *DECADES* composes a history of cinematic sound and score for each 20th century decade. The next installment will be the 1990s.

Her newest films are *BULK COLLECTION* (2022) and the ongoing music series *The Musicians* (2022).

Her writing on film, feminism, culture, and art has been featured in numerous anthologies, journals, and art catalogues such as *Bookforum*, *Artforum*, The Los Angeles Review of Books, *The Believer*, BOMB, *LitHub*, *Fence*, *Frieze*, *The New Inquiry*, *Berfrois*, *IndieWire*, *The White Review*, *Fireflies*, *The Rumpus*, *Performa 11*, and Pace Gallery. She has taught film, media, and literature at The New School, Pratt, and NYU.